GOD
IN
HEBREWS

ENCOUNTER WITH
GOD IN HEBREWS

JOY TETLEY

SERIES EDITORS
ALISON BARR, JOSEPHINE CAMPBELL, TONY HOBBS

SCRIPTURE UNION
130 CITY ROAD LONDON EC1V 2NJ

© Joy Tetley 1995

First published 1995

ISBN 0 86201 947 8

All rights reserved. No part of this publication may be reproduced, stored in a retrieval system, or transmitted, in any form or by any means, electronic, mechanical, photocopying, recording or otherwise, without the prior permission of Scripture Union.

The right of Joy Tetley to be identified as the author of this work has been asserted by her in accordance with the Copyright, Designs and Patents Act 1988.

Scripture quotations taken from the Holy Bible, New International Version. Copyright © 1973, 1978, 1984 by International Bible Society. Anglicisation copyright © 1979, 1984, 1989. Used by permission of Hodder and Stoughton Limited.

British Library Cataloguing-in-Publication Data
A catalogue record for this book is available from the British Library.

Cover design by Grax Design Consultants.

Phototypeset by Intype, London.

Printed and bound in Great Britain by Cox & Wyman Ltd, Reading, Berkshire.

CONTENTS

   Foreword   7
   Preface   10
1 To a community in crisis   13
2 This is our God   29
3 God with us   44
4 God of truth and promise   57
5 God of new beginnings   70
6 God of faith and commitment   85
7 Our priestly God   105
   Some questions to ponder and discuss   126

FOREWORD

Throughout its long history, promoting systematic, daily Bible reading has always been central to Scripture Union's world-wide ministry. At first there were Bible-reading cards that detailed a series of daily readings throughout the year. But before too long, comments were published to accompany the notes and, in the early 1920s, a quarterly booklet was produced. It was called *The Scripture Union* with the sub-title 'Daily Notes', the name by which the booklet was to become known.

By the 1920s Scripture Union's promotion of systematic daily Bible reading relied on three separate Bible-reading notes for the English-speaking world. Like *Daily Notes*, *Daily Bread* was widely used over several decades and these two were joined more recently by *Alive to God* which was launched to offer a complementary approach to Bible reading. All three publications have always had the following in common:

> A commitment to the authority and inspiration of biblical text;
> A conviction that reading the Bible should not merely be a cerebral process; readers should also be encouraged to respond to what they have read.

Bible-reading notes inevitably reflect the culture and concerns of their time. So, for example, some of the early notes made frequent attempts to summarise biblical passages using three points. Although this was a useful *aide-mémoire*, it did tend to be somewhat forced at times! More interestingly, the notes of the '30s, '40s and '50s – when the evangelical world was struggling with the impact of the implications of liberal scholarship – concentrated on re-stating the basic doctrinal truths. Today the notes reflect a strong emphasis on the importance of applying biblical principles and the growing interest throughout the Christian world on what can be described as 'spirituality'. This is seen in the increasingly varied forms of worship, the rediscovery of ancient Christian writing and music, and an awareness that responding to God can involve feelings and emotions as well as the mind.

There is much in Christian culture that is exciting and refreshing, but it is taking place against a background of a widespread decrease in Bible reading. It seems that the emphasis on Christian experience – important as that is – is blinding many people to the other side of the Christian life: duty and discipline. Twenty years ago most members of evangelical churches were committed to the importance of personal Bible reading on a regular basis. Nowadays, although many churches would claim to be Bible-based, individual members have all too often given up regular personal Bible reading. Bible-reading aids cannot in themselves change this trend. What we must continue to pray for is God's Holy Spirit to provoke whole Christian communities to rediscover the importance and excitement of regular Bible reading – without losing the joy of the variety and depth of Christian experience.

Marrying regular Bible reading with dynamic Christian

experience is the aim of Scripture Union Bible-reading notes. Partly to reflect that principle, it was recently decided to change the title of *Daily Notes* to *Encounter With God*. The former described the process but the latter describes the purpose.

Over the years readers have often encouraged us to reprint popular series of the notes. However, we have always been reluctant to do so, partly because writers prepare notes prayerfully and under the guidance of the Holy Spirit, for use at a particular time and in a particular way. Numerous stories from readers testify to how a particular note on a particular day met a specific need, and are witnesses to the Holy Spirit's role in the process. Nevertheless, when in the early 1990s we began to deal with entire biblical books in a single series, a formula began to suggest itself: not a reprinting of the series as such, but the series re-worked and expanded by the writer; still using the distinctive *Encounter With God* approach, but with the space to develop and explore some of the issues which could not be covered in a 300–word note.

There are a number of things that make Scripture Union Bible-reading notes distinctive, but one element perhaps stands out above all others: beginning and ending with scripture. Starting with the Bible passage, the writer offers thought-provoking comments to encourage the reader to go back to the passage with fresh enthusiasm and new insights, eager to respond with new commitment to what God is saying through scripture: in other words, *to encounter God*. It is the prayer of all who have worked on this series that such will be your experience as you read this book.

Tony Hobbs, Commissioning Editor
Adult Bible Reading Publications

PREFACE

The aim of this book is to open up a dialogue between the reader and the living God. There are few better vehicles for prompting such an exchange than the *Epistle to the Hebrews*. This powerful New Testament writing (so often avoided!) is nothing less than an urgent and compelling invitation to draw near to God – the God who longs for our company and who goes through hell to prove it.

The God we encounter in *Hebrews* is the God who in Jesus opens his heart to us; the God who through Jesus offers us a heart-to-heart relationship in which nothing is hidden and all can be forgiven. With this God we find our true home, our deepest fulfilment. With this God we can be ourselves. With this God we can face anything. By the grace and help of this God we can persevere against all the odds. In the presence of this God, whatever our condition, we can touch a profound joy which vibrates through eternity.

This is a God worth knowing. He will never fail us or forsake us. He is utterly faithful. And he asks nothing in return except responsive faithfulness. But here, of course, is the rub – as the first recipients of *Hebrews* were beginning to discover. A living relationship with a living God is no comfortable option. It bears a cost. It is risk and adventure and challenge. It brings no guarantee of earthly security. What it does bring is the sharing of God's life, God's companionship, God's understanding, God's resources. In the most fundamental sense, by holding on to this God, we come into our own. So claims *Hebrews*.

As we seek to meet with God by engaging with *Hebrews*, we shall undertake a journey: a journey of faith seeking understanding. We shall begin by exploring questions to do with the original context of the document. What sort of person and situation might have brought it into being? What kind of document is it? Then we shall embark on an expedition through the text, giving particular attention to the first two chapters where the author introduces his major themes. Next we shall reflect carefully on what we have discovered *en route* by examining the vision of God set before us in the Epistle as a whole (and it is very important to look at this writing as an integral unit). Finally, there will be some summary questions to stimulate further our thoughts and prayers.

Although close attention will be paid throughout the scriptural text, this book is not designed to provide a detailed, verse by verse, critical commentary. Neither will it set out in detail and weigh up at length the many scholarly views and interpretations that have grown up around the text. Books offering these should be consulted for the wealth of material they offer. The intention of this present little volume is rather more modest yet at the same time, perhaps, rather more audacious. It seeks (as *Hebrews* does) to deepen awareness of the living God and communication with that God. It seeks to break open a message which both disturbs and assures; a message which brings radical challenge yet radiates hope; a message which stirs up faith and courage, exploration and questioning; a message which invites us to live more closely and confidently with the God who 'says it all' in Jesus Christ.

Reading *Hebrews* in this spirit can change lives for good!

1
TO A COMMUNITY IN CRISIS

Hebrews is one of the most exciting and revolutionary books in the New Testament, not least in what it says about God, Jesus and priesthood. The theological implications of this document are little short of staggering. It is put together with an urgent passion which is both carefully argued and beautifully expressed. It has provided the Church with rich source material for liturgy and hymnody, not to mention a number of 'purple passages' dear to the hearts of many Christians. Yet, as a whole, over the centuries it has suffered a surprising lack of attention. In fact, for many Christians, *Hebrews* remains virtually a 'closed book'. There are no doubt a variety of reasons why this should be so, but one which is frequently expressed is that the language and thought of this Epistle are too complex and remote for people who are no longer in touch with the cultic and ritual concerns of first century Judaism. The impression is that the letter does not address the way we live now. Some, indeed, find its sacrificial terminology positively repulsive! Best, then, to give the book a wide berth and leave it to a handful of scholars.

It would be misleading to suggest that *Hebrews* is an easy or straightforward read. It is packed tight with meaning. But it is certainly not the case that this Epistle is either inaccessible or irrelevant to people today. Nothing could be further from the truth. Rather, this fascinating and challenging document invites us to share a vision which is of crucial importance, 'yesterday, today and for ever'.

To help us see the vision as clearly as possible, and so recognize its message for us, we shall look first at some background features which strongly influence the overall picture.

The writer

Unusually for an Epistle, the writer does not tell us his name (nor does he give any opening greetings). There has been no shortage of theories to supply the author's lack and deprive him of anonymity! Amongst candidates proposed are Barnabas, Apollos, Luke and Silvanus. You may wish to explore the cases put forward for these different candidates and those of others in the commentaries on *Hebrews*. Suffice to say that it is very unlikely indeed that Paul could have written *Hebrews*. The language, style and imagery found in this Epistle differ quite markedly from that we encounter in Paul's letters (though there are, of course, connections in faith and teaching). It seems that Paul's name became associated with *Hebrews* in the early centuries because it was felt that the writing must have apostolic authority to be canonically acceptable. An anonymous work would not do! It surely must be by Paul.

The matter of authorship cannot be finally settled. As Origen (a third century theologian) put it, 'Who wrote the Epistle to the Hebrews, God alone knows.' And, interesting though this issue is, *we* do not need to know. It is far more important to give our attention to the nameless writer's message, for it is a message that is God-inspired. Even biblical detective work can become escapism!

To a community in crisis

Nonetheless, whatever his precise identity, the text does offer us some strong indications as to the sort of person the writer was. (On balance of probability the writer was male, though as far back as the end of the nineteenth century Priscilla was brought into the reckoning as a candidate. In the culture of the time, female authorship would at least help to explain the work's anonymity. However, recognizing the greater likelihood that the author was a man, we shall use the masculine pronoun to refer to 'him'.)

Whenever we read books, we are in some way entering into a dialogue with the writers, for they have inevitably expressed much of themselves in their writings. That is no less true of biblical books, for God communicates with us through real people with their own personalities and contexts.

What, then, does this text suggest about its human author? First, that he was a person to whom worship meant a great deal. His writing is permeated by the language and ethos of worship: by words such as 'draw near', 'offer', 'contemplate', 'make intercession'; by notions such as priesthood, sacrifice and heavenly worship. The whole text is shot through with an evocation of the liturgical. The whole text invites a response of worshipful commitment and obedience. And its insistent call to consider, contemplate and look into Jesus, strongly suggests that the author himself was given to such active pondering and reflection. His writing gives us the distinct impression that here was someone who practised what he preached.

Much of the language and imagery that he uses draws on the worship practices (and attitudes) of the Jewish people, particularly in relation to the offering of sacrifice to a holy God. He makes reference to a wide range of sacrificial rituals, but the one which he puts under the

15

spotlight from a Christian point of view is that connected with the Day of Atonement. As an aid to understanding what he is trying to communicate by focussing on this ceremony, it would be well worth reading in advance a passage such as Leviticus 16. In fact, glancing through the whole of *Leviticus* would stir up an awareness of the kind of context Hebrews was working in, just as re-acquainting oneself with *Deuteronomy* would foster understanding of what he says concerning the holy covenant God.

It must certainly be the case that both the writer and his community were familiar with the provisions for worship made in the Jewish scriptures. In all probability they were themselves Jewish converts to the way of Jesus. But it is interesting that the writer concentrates his attention on liturgical arrangements as set out in writings from the Pentateuch (the first five books of the Old Testament). These provisions for approaching God relate to the time after the Exodus when God's people were wandering in the wilderness as they journeyed painfully to the Promised Land. It is the worship of Tabernacle rather than Jewish Temple which Hebrews uses by way of illustration, comparison and contrast. Theologically, this fits well with his concern that the new covenant people of God should be a people on the move, a people who have no 'abiding city', a people travelling to their promised rest with God. It also enables him to emphasize how Jesus, the 'pioneer' leader far greater than Moses (Hebrews 3:1–6), brings to their end (ie their true fulfilment) all the careful provisions made to enable sinful human beings to have safe communion with the living God.

But, at the same time, using such imagery may suggest that the author and recipients of *Hebrews* were not based in or near Jerusalem, nor were they then or in the past regular participants in Temple worship. If they had been, then a perceptive writer like Hebrews would very likely have exploited that situation by addressing it directly in relation to the work of Christ. This would still apply if, by the time of writing, the Jerusalem Temple had been destroyed. (Incidentally, wherever he was situated, Hebrews would surely have taken advantage of the fall of the Temple; pointing to that would have strongly reinforced his argument. That he does not seems a persuasive reason for dating the Epistle before AD 70.) The likeliest scenario is that the Epistle's recipients were Jewish Christians who knew their scriptures and valued their traditions; so much so that, with the onset of other severe pressures, they were being tempted to abandon the blessings and consequences of the new covenant.

With his pervasive emphasis on worship, the author of *Hebrews* touches on the heart of things: for himself, for his community, and for us. It is through worship that we most deeply apprehend the truth of God.

To Hebrews, God meant everything. His writing is characterized by its theocentricity, its God-centredness. God is the dominant subject throughout. And what a God! A God of paradox – 'a consuming fire' (12:29), to whom vengeance belongs (10:30), and who must be worshipped with reverence and awe. A living God, into whose hands it is a fearful thing to fall: yet, *at the same time*, the source of tender mercy and grace, who can be approached with confident boldness and complete freedom of speech. The God of encouragement, commitment and utter faithfulness. This God is a God of passion, in every sense of the phrase. He has strong feelings. He yearns for his people. He suffers with them and for them. Though the word 'love' is not used of God in *Hebrews*, the reality of divine love sears through the whole Epistle. It is not the abstract love of controlled detachment. It is not platonic. It is fully involved and full-blooded. It is the fierce yet tender love of the God of the covenant, expressed so graphically in Old Testament writings like *Deuteronomy* and the prophets. For Hebrews, though the details of the covenant might change, the character of the covenant God does not. Yet Hebrews has come to realize that God's passionate love has one supreme focus: the one who is God's comprehensive self-expression, the one through whom the divine paradox can be most fruitfully experienced. Jesus.

With all his uncompromising theocentricity, Hebrews was clearly devoted to Jesus. He uses the name 'Jesus', usually without qualification, over a dozen times, and it invariably comes in an emphatic position at the beginning or end of a phrase. That is not always clear from English translations. So, for example, that familiar phrase contained in 12:2, which is usually translated something like 'looking to Jesus the pioneer and perfecter of our faith', reads literally, 'looking away into the pioneer and perfecter of our faith, Jesus'. Hebrews had obviously been captivated by Jesus and enjoyed a living and active relationship with him. But where did that leave his God-centredness? Where did it leave that monotheism so fundamental to his faith as a Jew? His ongoing experience of Jesus, and his reflection on that experience, pushed him out into deep theological waters, and out of those depths has come one of the most adventurous and creative writings of the New Testament. As we shall see, what he has to say is decidedly radical, and has far-reaching consequences for an understanding of the way God is and the way God works.

Our author, then, is a bold and creative theologian,

To a community in crisis

whose theology is born of religious experience and reflection. He is not a detached academic. He starts with a committed faith, a faith which goes on to seek understanding. He is totally involved with his material for, in his view, it is not there simply to provide an opportunity for an interesting intellectual exercise – it is a matter of life and death.

It is clear, too, that the writer is very inclusive in his understanding of God as seen in Jesus. As there are many aspects to the divine, so there are many ways of apprehending the mystery who is Jesus. He is, amongst other things, God's wisdom, God's mouthpiece, God's Word, God's servant, God's true Adam, God's eternal Son; and he is for *everyone*, of that the author has no doubt. Above all, for our author, Jesus is the human expression of God's priesthood. Perceiving Jesus as priest – as the expression of God's priesthood – is something unique to the author of *Hebrews* amongst New Testament writers. Only he explicitly expounds the significance of Jesus in these terms (though other New Testament writers use language and imagery that has the potential to become a priestly picture). It is most likely that Hebrews came to his apprehension (as we might say, the penny dropped) in the context of (Christian) worship. Priesthood is, after all, a very liturgical image. For Hebrews, it drew together many ways of looking at Jesus, and implied astounding things about God. It was a vision he felt impelled to share.

The way he does it is powerfully effective. Stylistically, Hebrews' work is carefully organized, carefully expressed and characterized by a carefully argued enthusiasm. He does not let his enthusiasm run away with him or tie him in knots (Paul sometimes seems to have more difficulty curbing his!). But he *is* an enthusiast (in the literal sense of one 'fired by God'). Yet his use of the Greek language and his rhetorical technique are excellent. Hebrews is a splendid example of how rigorous thinking, strong feeling and deep spiritual commitment can be fruitfully combined in a striking work of communication. The power of his writing certainly owes much to his keenly poetic sensitivity. We have only to look at the Epistle's opening chapter to appreciate that. Whatever raw materials the author was using, he has created a theological poem of awesome beauty and intensity. It has a profound impact, whether or not we do any detailed theological analysis of its constituent parts.

In the light of all that has been said so far, it is no surprise to realize that, in all likelihood, Hebrews was essentially a preacher. He calls his work a 'word of exhortation' (13:22), almost a technical term in the New Testament for a homily (*cf* Acts 13:15). In fact, what we are doing when we read *Hebrews* is listening to a sermon. For those with a Jewish synagogue background, Hebrews' preaching method would be a familiar one: the weaving together of a variety of scriptural texts (one or two of which may have been set readings for the day) with expository comment. The sermon is about an hour long, short by first century standards!

We learn from Philo (a Jewish philosopher) that in the Jewish synagogue the scripture exposition on a Sabbath could go on for much of the day (with a lunch break!), and Josephus (a Jewish historian) also suggests that a Sabbath day in the synagogue could mean quite literally that. A glance at Acts 20:7–12 indicates that Christian assemblies and sermons (perhaps modelled on those of the synagogue) could also last for some considerable time. By Paul's standards at Troas, Hebrews' word of encouragement was indeed brief, as he reminds his congregation (13:22). There are, in fact, broad hints in his exposition that he could have said much more (eg 'But we cannot discuss these things in detail now', 9:5b). Perhaps he shortened his homily to what he considered to be absolutely essential because he knew that much of his teaching would be hard to take in (*cf* 5:11ff). It was something people had to 'bear with' (13:22). It is nonetheless clear that this preacher does not force-feed his community with material that is deliberately academic and obscure. What he offers them is not a sophisticated diet to be taken as an optional extra; he gives them what he regards as integral and vital to their survival and growth as Christians.

As a preacher, Hebrews has a deep and urgent pastoral concern for the members of his community. He feels them to be in a dangerous spiritual condition, and he feels constrained to say so in no uncertain terms. He speaks what is in many ways a hard prophetic word to his community, yet that word is infused with the passion of real caring – a longing that his beloved brothers and sisters should grow into maturity and move on towards the joy that was set before them. Like the God he worships, he is passionately concerned, and, at times, this leads him to use strong language. Nonetheless, being a good pastor and preacher, he invariably follows such language with words of encouragement (eg 6:4–11). And more often than not he uses the first person plural, thus including himself in his exhortations. He also starts where his people are, by using a good deal of material that would be familiar to them. Typically, however, he uses much of that material in a surprising way, thus demanding from his congregation a radical shift in perspective, a new way of seeing. As *we* shall see, this facility is well illustrated by the way he tackles the priesthood of Jesus. In the methodology of his preaching, as well as in its content, Hebrews makes no concessions to that 'laziness' he regards as a major spiritual danger (eg 6:12).

But by what right did he address this community with such firm authority? How did he stand in relation to them? At the time of writing he is away (13:19,23); and he assumes, without evident request or apology, that he can preach to them without going through their leaders. Those leaders are mentioned only at the end (13:7,17,24), and then not addressed directly. They may not even have been present at this assembly. We will touch on this again later.

To sum up, then. We cannot identify the preacher's name, and we cannot be certain of his precise relationship with the people to whom he is writing. What *is* clear, however, is that he speaks with spiritual authority and from a close awareness of the community's context and conditions.

The community addressed

To whom was this 'meaty' sermon directed? Again, the only definite answer is that we do not know! There are many interesting theories (of which the commentaries will provide full details). Most commentators locate the community away from Jerusalem, or even outside Palestine, whilst arguing that the people addressed do have a Jewish background. The language and approach of the sermon would seem to be most appropriate for Christian converts who were Hellenistic Jews of the Dispersion. That is to say that they would be from a Jewish community somewhere in the Greek-speaking world (a phrase which could be applied to many places in the Roman Empire!). In scholarly terms, popular suggestions include Alexandria, Corinth or Rome. The latter has the most weight of tradition behind it and can still muster a very strong case. Perhaps as a working hypothesis we can assume that Hebrews' word of encouragement was addressed to a group of Jewish Christians in Rome in the mid-60s of the first century AD – a time and place of great danger and testing for followers of Jesus. The emperor Nero was on the scene, with all his strange and cruel designs. His persecution of Christians following the (imperially instigated?) fire of Rome was, to say the least, horrific.

Certainly the text suggests that the Hebrews community was facing the real danger of severe persecution and, consequently, was being tempted to fall back into the safety of some form of Judaism. We need to bear in mind that from the point of view of the secular authorities Christianity was not yet a recognized religion, and attitudes towards the adherents of Jesus could vary enormously and turn nasty very quickly (as we see, for example, from the Acts of the Apostles). Being a Christian was not a recipe for earthly security. Being a Jew (for the most part, rebellious opposition excepted) offered rather more protection.

The Christians addressed by Hebrews were clearly living in testing times. But it seems they have not yet reached the point of having to shed their blood in order to be faithful to Jesus (12:3–4). Hardship and hostility, however, were very much in evidence, and (in the preacher's view) they were not coping with these very effectively. They had lost the fire and strength of their first love when their faith had enabled them to stand firm against and even be joyful about opposition. 'Remember those earlier days,' says the preacher, 'when you stood your ground in a great contest in the face of suffering. Sometimes you were publicly exposed to insult and persecution; at other times you stood side by side with those who were so treated. You sympathized with those in prison and joyfully accepted the confiscation of your property, because you knew that you yourselves had better and lasting possessions' (10:32–34). And now? Now the heart seemed to have gone out of them. Metaphorically (and perhaps physically!) their arms were 'feeble' and their knees 'weak' (12:12). 'Take hold on yourselves and your faith,' exhorts the preacher. 'You have even now a tremendous privilege *and* a glorious future. Don't throw it all away.'

What had occasioned this sad decline in faith? What had unnerved them? If they could face serious danger in earlier times, why not now? Of course, we can only speculate. But there is one possibility, very compatible with the text and tenor of the sermon, that might be worth considering. Could it be that this group of Christians, once through their early testing, had come to concentrate on what we might call an 'exaltation spirituality' – a triumphalist emphasis on the sovereign lordship of Christ and the exalted status of his followers? Christ had delivered them. This they believed and this they proclaimed. But a second, and perhaps more severe, bout of opposition, coupled with the real possibility of torture and bloodletting, had shaken this victorious approach to the roots. Doubts, fears and questioning were replacing easy complacency. This time Jesus did not seem to be ready with deliverance. Was Jesus not a heavenly king after all? If he was, why did he not use his power and intervene on behalf of his own? Was it rather that God was displeased with them for glorifying Jesus and neglecting the traditional means of approaching and worshipping the one and only

Lord? Was their experience thus to be interpreted as divine retribution, akin to the way God had dealt with his erring people of old? Our preacher seeks to meet this situation by stressing that Jesus is indeed Lord and King – even more glorious than they had realized – the very self-expression of God himself. Yet his divine majesty and glory, the essential characteristics of his power, are to be perceived at their truest in humiliation, testing and death. It is rejection of this *new* covenant revelation which is the real spiritual danger. How shall they escape if they neglect such a great salvation? The path into that saving glory has to be the path that Jesus trod.

There is no doubt that, whatever the precise spiritual condition of the people addressed, the preacher of *Hebrews* is urgently concerned to keep them on course and to exhort them to grow through their difficulties into a more mature understanding of God, to become more committed to the Christian life. They are a people in crisis. To meet that crisis they must practise steadfast endurance, remaining utterly faithful to the God of the new covenant. They are indeed right to focus on Jesus at God's right hand, but they need to ponder far more deeply what that exalted position really says about God and about Jesus – and, in consequence, about their own vocation as Christian disciples.

The preacher's 'big idea'

People are often more able to grasp the essence of a difficult message if it is focussed in one striking and memorable image. The wavering Christians addressed by Hebrews are certainly presented with that. Their teacher had a 'picture' to share which he hoped would bring home his urgent message. It was not just a sermon illustration. It was a picture that for him exposed the very heart of God.

Hebrews' burning conviction of the absolute primacy of God, his personal experience of God through and in Jesus, his attraction to worship, his Jewish background and knowledge of Christian teaching, and his concern for a Christian community under threat, all come together as, in the context of worship, he begins to see Jesus as the great high priest. Jesus is crowned with glory and honour, but so crowned *because of* the sacrificial suffering of death. This insight expresses so well and in such an integrated way what Hebrews felt about God and his relationship with humankind. The essence of priesthood was to bring God and humanity together. It was precisely this, believed Hebrews, that Jesus had done to perfection – and he had done so as the self-expression of God, as the human expression of God's eternal Son and as new Adam (1 Corinthians 15:45). Those two 'images of God' were inextricably bound together in the human, dying and exalted Jesus. So the priestly work of Jesus issued from the direct action of God. Such was our preacher's perception. Pondering on it made him realize that it implied astounding things about God. Without in any way diminishing his holiness (a quality in fact underlined by the priestly image), God enters fully into the human condition, lives a life that is 'faithful unto death' and 'offers' his death as the expiation for sin and the inauguration of a new covenant. In so doing, he redefines both priesthood and sacrifice. Priesthood breaks dramatically out of its Jewish limits and sacrifice becomes not 'the blood of bulls and goats' but the offering of a totally obedient and consecrated life (*cf* 10:3–10). Further, in Hebrews' vision priesthood and sacrifice become one. The consecrated life offered is that of the high priest himself – and the high priest is the one through whom God created the world, who upholds the universe by the word of his power and in whom God speaks his definitive word (*cf* 1:1–3).

It is a daring picture, and one which draws together the preacher's God-centredness and devotion to Jesus. It also powerfully portrays the message he longs to get across to his community. God has focussed his priestly concern in Jesus his Son, releasing humanity from the burden of sin and death and making possible that union with him which is both rest and re-creation. Yet this could not be achieved without much suffering. It required self-offering to an ultimate degree. There could be no glory without passion. The brothers and sisters of Jesus must digest this very carefully. They could not repeat the sacrifice of the great high priest but, in entering into their salvation, they should expect hostility from those who refuse to accept God's word. They must regard this hostility positively, as divine training appropriate to privileged children on the way to glory (*cf* 12:2ff). Even Jesus had to be made perfect through suffering (2:10; 5:8–9). They must keep looking to him and then, despite and through everything, they would know real joy.

Hebrews composes this message carefully into a homily designed to be read out to the community assembled for worship. Perhaps that worship consisted of the breaking of bread, the Lord's Supper. If so, that would add particular point and poignancy to Hebrews' stress on the bringing in of a new covenant though the blood of Jesus (see Matthew 26:27–28; Mark 14:23–24; Luke 22:20; 1 Corinthians 11:25–26).

Whoever the writer of *Hebrews* was, whatever it was precisely that prompted his sermon, what he has given us is a work of penetrating significance. Exploring it offers us the rich opportunity of an in-depth conversation with the living God. So let us begin our journey – and our dialogue.

2
THIS IS OUR GOD

Hebrews 1:1 – 2:4

An overture

Hebrews has a great deal to share with the people he cares about so much. He knows that a significant part of what he has to say may well prove unpalatable. Yet he is convinced that it has to be said. The spiritual survival of this community may depend on it. So it is crucial that his urgent message comes across in the most effective way possible. His text suggests that he has thought very carefully about its presentation. He wants to expose the heart of the matter in a way that will reach the heart of a people in crisis. He wants them to experience afresh the saving passion of a living, faithful God. He wants to rekindle their hope and their courage. He wants to renew and deepen their relationship with a God who gives everything for love of them, who longs to share with them his very life.

This is a daunting agenda; all the more so because the people concerned are not likely to be easily convinced. Their immature and crumbling faith is not best placed to receive a word which hurts and challenges even as it strengthens and builds up. Their perception of God needs to be broadened and deepened at a time when fear and despair are crouching at the door. At such times, people crave for familiarity and security, even when those desirables are, in reality, profoundly damaging. The Hebrews community is no exception. Yet the preacher who addresses them believes passionately that the only faithful way through this dilemma is to move forward, not back; to break new ground in understanding and commitment. He has no illusions as to how hard this will be. But he wants to demonstrate powerfully to them that moving on with the God of Jesus Christ means coming into their own. It means discovering, though not without pain, salvation that is comprehensive and eternal, and pursuing a relationship which, though stormy, will be the making of them.

Being the consummate preacher that he is, Hebrews is aware of the importance of beginning well. The opening section of his exhortation (chapters 1 and 2) is carefully designed to engage the attention and prepare the way for what is to follow. Effectively, it is an overture in which the composer's main themes are introduced and rehearsed. The original hearers would recognize much here that was familiar. The material would strike chords, both in the realm of ideas and the realm of experience. Yet they would also have to come to terms with new sounds as well as fresh ways of playing old melodies. By the time the overture ends (2:18), we can imagine an audience both encouraged and disturbed, dispirited and apprehensive, yet feeling the first deep stirrings of hope. Whatever their response they will undoubtedly have been made to listen.

An opening sentence

The first sentence of *Hebrews* covers the whole of verses 1–4 in our English translations. It is an arresting, not to say astounding, introduction. And its whole focus (like that of the entire work) is on God. Here the preacher gives a vivid verbal portrait of the God who means everything to him, the God who is the source and substance of the urgent message he seeks to share.

From the outset, Hebrews makes it clear that the God who asks for commitment does so as one who is totally committed to that which he has brought into being. Awesome this God most certainly is. Remote and detached he most certainly is not. This is a God determined to communicate, a God who takes the initiative, a God given to creativity and self-expression. Many-splendoured variety is characteristic of God's way of working, for this God is maker of all things and sovereign over all things. And at the eternal heart of this God's being is relationship: at the eternal heart of this God's being is one who is a Son, one who shares in the great enterprise of creating and sustaining the universe, one who can perfectly reveal the divine nature.

It is this Son who, in becoming human, is for humanity the focal and ultimate expression of who God is and how God works. The writer of *Hebrews* wants his audience to be in no doubt that when they look to the Son, they see into the life of God. Already, in this concentrated opening sentence, there is a wealth of significance to explore. So, for example, the eternal Son is spoken of in language used by Jewish writers to describe God's Wisdom (Hebrews 1:2–3; compare especially Proverbs 8:22–31; and in the Apocrypha, Wisdom of Solomon 7:24–27). The same Greek word (*apaugasma*) is used to describe the Son as 'the radiance of God's glory' (Hebrews 1:3) and Wisdom as 'reflection of eternal light' (in Wisdom of Solomon 7:26). If, as seems likely, the Hebrews community were predominantly Jews with a Hellenistic background, they would warm to this presentation of God's Son. The figure of Wisdom (*Sophia*) had come to express in poetic form the active relationship between God and creation. Wisdom is presented as the personification of God's attitude towards and involvement with the created order. It is a striking, suggestive metaphor and, for those bound to strict monotheism, a daring one. If taken too literally, Wisdom could be seen as a separate divine being, someone who acts as an intermediary between God and the world. Yet there is, perhaps, in this picture of *Sophia* an intuitive awareness of variety and inter-relatedness (even femininity) within the one God. And Wisdom is a very attractive figure, vibrant with creative life, one who conveys both delight and authority, one who opens up and shares the workings of God, one who is exalted with God. (Wisdom of Solomon 6:12 – 10:21 gives a vivid impression of her qualities.)

It is not surprising that what is said about God's Wisdom comes to be seen by many early Christians as highly applicable to Jesus (eg John 1:1–11; 1 Corinthians 8:6; Colossians 1:15–19; Revelation 3:14). The 'Jesus experience' was overwhelming and comprehensive in its transforming power. Jesus excited praise, devotion and commitment. Jesus was experienced as vitally present, one with whom relationship could be enjoyed. Jesus brought challenge and liberation, not as a significant yet dead example from the recent past, but as someone very much alive with the life of God. How, then, was the reality of this experience to be integrated with exclusive allegiance to the one God? The insights of Wisdom poetry helped to open up a way of understanding that went beyond the picture language of *Sophia*. In trying to express the significance of the living God who had taken hold of them,

Christians began to explore Jesus' relationship with the living God, and to explore it in terms of person rather than personification. For Jesus was not just a poetic perception. He had been a flesh and blood human being. Yet he produced God-like effects, and not only during his time on earth. So what on earth – and in heaven – was to be made of him?

For Hebrews, as for the other New Testament writers, this was no academic question. It was the most important issue in life. It mattered profoundly. It still does. Hebrews himself was convinced that the Son of whom he speaks in the opening sentence 'bears the very stamp of God's nature' (RSV) in being the one through whom God created the world, the one who upholds all things 'by his word of power' (RSV). Here is divine wisdom indeed, but in the form of a real person rather than merely as an attribute of God. The one God, it seems, is a more complex unity than orthodox Jewish monotheism might have envisaged.

An emphatic part of the message of *Hebrews* is that God's Son (clearly identified in 2:9 as the one called Jesus) is greater in status than any other figure in Jewish tradition. Hebrews will stress that God's Son is superior to Moses, Aaron and Joshua. Here in the opening sentence, he presents the Son as God's supreme Prophet (1:2a), not only God's mouthpiece but the very embodiment of God's word. And the Son is exalted and honoured as divine King (v3c), on a par with the majesty of God (this is an allusion – the first of many – to Psalm 110, a psalm of considerable importance in *Hebrews*). Even spiritual beings cannot compare with the Son. As Son, he has a more excellent name than the angels (v4), a name which discloses the divine nature of his person, a name he possesses by hereditary right. (The NIV is right to translate as 'inherited' the word which is rendered 'obtained' in other versions.)

There is still more to take in and ponder. It may well be that in 1:3 Hebrews is quoting a Christian hymn already used in worship (akin to those that might be contained in Colossians 1:15–20 and Philippians 2:6–11). It is, after all, good preaching technique to refer to the other elements in a service! Certainly verse 3 can be set out as a poetic stanza:

> who is (the) radiance of God's glory
> and (the) stamp* of his being
> sustaining all things by his powerful word.

[*'exact representation' in NIV translation]

It also follows a pattern, discernible in the other New Testament passages that affirm the significance of Christ, which might be particularly appropriate in a worship setting (especially Philippians 2:6ff). That pattern is exaltation, humiliation, glory (and carries a distinct echo of the experience of the Suffering Servant as presented in Isaiah 52:13 – 53:12). But if Hebrews is quoting a known hymn in praise of Christ, he is also amending it. For verse 3 contains the first hint of a theme that will be richly expounded in the writer's subsequent exhortation, a theme unique to *Hebrews*, a theme with radical implications. In declaring that the Son 'provided purification [cleansing] for sins', the writer prepares us for encountering the Son (the 'exact representation of God') as priest. In Jewish law, making purification for sins was the business of the priest. If the Son fully expresses God's word, he also expresses the saving nature of God's priesthood. This is a truth which the Hebrews community, and we ourselves, will have to explore very carefully. We could begin by engaging with the implications of this little phrase tucked away in verse 3. Through God's Son, we are to understand that the great God of heaven is the one who reaches out to cleanse soiled humanity from the clinging dirt of sin. In order, humbly, to wash us clean, God is more than willing to get his hands dirty. It is a moving tender picture and one that has vital things to say about the essential (if paradoxical) character of the living God.

By the end of Hebrews' first sentence, members of the community have been powerfully reminded of the greatness of God and the significance of his Son. They have also been challenged to think more deeply, to push at the boundaries of their understanding, to see things in a new perspective. And all this not merely to give them a stimulus to theological reflection, but to set a context in which the importance of holding to this God is far more compelling than the temporary alleviation of earthly problems.

God's Son is the greatest!

Having hit them hard at the outset, Hebrews now hammers home to his community the absolute supremacy of the Son. Even with the angels, there is no contest.

In the Judaism of the New Testament period, angels enjoyed something of a high profile. They were part of the heavenly worshipping community, included in the counsels of God, involved in the oversight of the affairs of nations and the care of individuals. They were God's messengers and agents of revelation. It was also believed that angels were mediators of the covenant to Moses on Mt Sinai. In the more mystical and esoteric strains of Judaism, they were regarded as intermediaries (not to say obstacles) between God and the aspiring mystic. They could, of course, be malevolent as well as benevolent.

Whatever the Hebrews community believed about angels, they needed to be decisively reminded that God's Son was more than angelic. In his sermon as a whole, the writer stresses that Jesus, the Son of God, is the mediator of a new covenant, the one who is the message as well as the messenger, the one who opens up in his own person the very presence of God. At this point (1:5-14), Hebrews uses a string of Old Testament quotations (drawn from the Greek version of the Old Testament) to demonstrate the primacy of God's Son. These would have had a considerable impact on the Jewish Christians the preacher was addressing. Even today in our own age and culture, these verses, and their cumulative effect, are a force to be reckoned with. They are meant to make a deep and challenging impression. They succeed in their purpose.

Some of the Jewish scriptures used here would be familiar to the recipients as Christian *testimonia* – passages believed to bear witness to and be fulfilled by the coming of Jesus Christ. So it would be with Psalm 2:7 (Hebrews 1:5a; *cf* Acts 13:33) and Psalm 110:1 (Hebrews 1:13; *cf* Acts 2:34–35). Others they may not have thought of in this way before. It would be typical of the preacher of *Hebrews* to mix the familiar with the new.

He presents all the passages as spoken directly by God to the Son or of the Son, and therefore of incontrovertible authority. What God thereby declares (1:5) is not just an interesting idea; it is a truth that requires a response of bold faith, worship and commitment. For God's Son is much more than the righteous messianic king, the anointed one of Jewish expectation (vv8–9). He is divine – addressed by God as God. This is the most obvious reading of verse

8. (The relevant phrase could also be translated 'God is your throne...' or 'Your throne is God...', but these possibilities would take some explaining, particularly when in the same opening section the writer is presenting a theological picture of the Son seated *at God's right hand* (v13). That image is easier to appreciate than the notion of the Son sitting *on* God!) Hebrews has already set forward the Son not only as heir of all things and agent and sustainer of creation but also as 'the radiance of God's glory and the exact representation of his being'. Taken together, these descriptions add up to an impressive testimony to the Son's divine credentials. It is not such an unthinkable step from here to call the Son 'God' explicitly. This is especially so, perhaps, if the primary context for Hebrews' use of the psalm is that of worship. The experience of worship not infrequently opens up new horizons with which doctrinal thinking then has to engage. We may recall Thomas's adoring response to the risen Christ in John 20:28, 'My Lord and my God'.

Certainly it is clear from the whole text of *Hebrews* that worship is regarded by the author as vitally important. As we have seen, the language and ethos of worship permeate the Epistle and are central to its climax (*cf* 12:28). We must give God his due, in honesty, reverence and awe. And that means we must give close and dedicated attention to God's Son.

Not only can the Son be addressed as God. Things spoken of by God under the old covenant can now be seen as descriptive of the Son (1:10–12). So the Son is responsible for creation and, unlike that order, remains eternally the same (*cf* 13:8). If the ministering angels are bidden to worship him (v6), how much more should we!

As if all this were not enough to assimilate, something

else is going on in this section, something which later on in the sermon will prove both important and very hard to cope with. Eventually, Hebrews wants to assert that the Son's priesthood is after the order of Melchizedek. He knows this will be difficult. So he includes some underlying preparation in his use of Psalm 45:6–7 (*cf* Hebrews 1:8, 9). Melchizedek, he will remind his listeners in chapter 7, means 'king of righteousness'. The royal figure in the psalm quotation loves righteousness and has a sceptre of righteousness as the sceptre of his kingdom. Near the beginning of the preacher's exhortation, he has slipped in something that is subtly suggestive of the mysterious Melchizedek. Thus he alerts the sub-conscious to what is to come later, he prepares the way for a shock.

Towards a surprising God

From his opening section we can see that Hebrews is a skilful and effective communicator. It is also clear that he is someone who believes what he says. And what he says points compellingly to a sovereign God who, with and in his Son, takes responsibility for creation, both in its origins and in its subsequent fallenness. As Hebrews will soon show, we either deny this commitment of God to his creation or affirm its truth wholeheartedly with life-changing consequences. There must be no half-measures in responding to a totally committed God.

The character of God's commitment is further explored in the next section of the preacher's overture (chapter 2). Now the theme becomes even more challenging, with the potential to reach right down into the depths of human experience. There, says Hebrews, can God be found and known. For the God of majesty, authority and glory has deliberately embraced weakness, tasting suffering and death in order to offer humanity a way through to freedom, hope and fulfilment. That is not an easy message to accept, either then or now. It does not sit comfortably with a triumphalist emphasis that sees faith as dispensing with all problems, so producing a constant feel-good factor for the believer. But Hebrews' message does take seriously the reality of fear and pain. As the Hebrews community needed to learn afresh, it is a message that goes to the true heart of things, even in the midst of hardship and loss. It is in this context that the nature of God's power and victory is most effectively realized.

A spiritual health warning

The writer of *Hebrews* is both a stirring preacher and a caring pastor. Because of his urgent concern for the spiritual health of his community, he does not hesitate to issue strong and chilling warnings about the dangers of drifting away from faith. There is too much to be lost! People must be brought to realize the critical nature of their condition.

The congregation have just been forcefully reminded of the greatness of God and the imperative to hold God's Son in the highest honour. In this first of his uncompromising 'warning passages' (2:1–4; *cf* 6:1–12; 10:26–39), the preacher emphasizes that any slipping away from commitment to this God must meet with dire consequences. Breaking the old covenant ('the message declared through angels') incurred severe penalties. How much worse for those who transgress the new covenant, that 'great salvation' declared through 'the Lord', to which God bore witness in striking ways.

For Hebrews, there is a real and significant continuity between the covenants, a continuity expressed not in outward form (the new, as will be stressed, is different) but in the changeless character of the covenant God. God's reasons for bringing these covenants into being are the same – he wants a closer relationship with humanity. The same God who spoke of old has spoken in one who is his Son (1:1–2). Yet he is still a holy God, 'a consuming fire' (12:29). It is a fearful thing to fall into his hands (10:31), particularly if one has spurned his greatest act of grace. To Hebrews, this is a matter of the utmost urgency. It is the living, active and heart-searching God with whom God's people have to deal (4:12–13). Both they and the preacher must give this their full and careful attention (2:1).

The tone of this section, like much of Hebrews' writing, is reminiscent of *Deuteronomy*. Obedience and loyalty bring blessing (Deuteronomy 28:1) Disobedience and betrayal bring alienation from God, with distressing consequences (Deuteronomy 28:15) For the writer of *Deuteronomy*, as for the author of *Hebrews*, the verb 'to hear' is a very strong one. 'Hearing' demands a response of obedience. What the Hebrews community have heard (Hebrews 2:1) concerns a covenant to end all covenants. To enjoy its benefits, they must hold fast to its terms.

As Hebrews will underline in his exposition, those terms are not burdensome (*cf* 1 John 5:3). They involve not a set of rules but staying true to a personal relationship with a living (and tantalizing) God. This will not always mean a comfortable, trouble-free life. It *will* mean a partnership that, together, can face anything; a partnership whose purpose is the discovery (often through painful experience) of eternal joy beyond imagining. Such a partnership is worth holding on to, whatever the pressures.

The significance of this new covenant relationship should have been apparent to the Hebrews community. Not only did they have the testimony of those who had heard the Lord (ie Jesus, 2:3), they had also experienced signs and wonders and acts of power brought about by God, and the effects among them of various gifts of the Holy Spirit (v4). What more did they want to convince them?

The phrases used here are of considerable interest. The word translated 'miracles' in NIV (literally, 'powerful deeds') is a word much used in the Synoptic Gospels (Matthew, Mark and Luke) to describe the mighty works of Jesus, done in the power of God and pointing to the character of God's kingdom. 'Signs and wonders' are certainly not confined to *Hebrews*. The phrase occurs 15 times in the New Testament, 9 of these references being in the Acts of the Apostles. In a minority of cases (Matthew 24:24; Mark 13:22; John 4:48) there is a warning against putting too much reliance on such phenomena. They can detract from faith and, indeed, be counterfeit. But the emphasis in New Testament usage is on signs and wonders as appropriate to the activity of God. And, as in *Hebrews*, they are particularly linked with the Holy Spirit.

But what are they for? The Old Testament can give us a pointer which is of particular significance for Hebrews. Here the majority of the 24 references to signs and wonders (10 of which are in *Deuteronomy*) are related to the Exodus, God's deliverance of his people from Egypt. God performed mighty works in the saving of his people. It is perhaps not surprising that the author of *Hebrews* should highlight the divine testimony of 'signs and wonders' in relation to an even greater act of salvation. They are not to be focussed on for their own sake but as indicators that the new covenant is truly of God. Signs direct attention to God, wonders evoke a response of awe and worship, and mighty acts display God's power. But they are not God. And they are not the whole story about God. God's greatest sign, God's greatest wonder, is to be discerned in one who, in the days of his flesh, knew failure as well as victory, one for whom triumph came *out of* – rather than instead of – tragedy.

This disturbing section is a challenging and timely message for the Jewish Christians addressed by Hebrews. It seems they were being strongly tempted to retreat into the securities of the past, into the relative safety of the old covenant, probably under the pressure of threatened persecution. Perhaps they were disillusioned that God did not now appear to be coming to their aid with spectacular acts. Was he angry with them? Had they been wrong to put their faith in a 'new' covenant when what God demanded was allegiance to what had been? Was Christian faith, anyway, worth the cost of all these problems? We may understand their wavering and confusion at a very difficult time. What they needed to put them on track, believed Hebrews, was to re-discover and re-affirm the profound wonder and surprising reality of God's good news.

All this is a salutary reminder for us of the tremendous treasure we have through God's divine and costly work of salvation. If we allow that treasure to slip through our hands, we shall be infinitely poorer, for we shall be letting go of blessings and benefits that no-one and nothing else can provide. We shall be denying ourselves the inestimable privilege of sharing the life of God. Taking hold of this privilege may well mean a difficult break with the past; it may well mean facing ridicule, and painful questions. But it also means that we shall live with God for ever. The positive joy of that will ultimately redeem and transfigure every negative.

3

GOD WITH US

Hebrews 2:5–18

Seeing Jesus

If Hebrews has just put the fear of God into his hearers, he now invites them to contemplate more closely the God to whom obedience is due. To do that, they must 'see Jesus' (2:9).

It is not until this point in the exposition that the incomparable and divine Son of God is named for the first time as Jesus. This name is clearly of great significance for the author of *Hebrews*. He uses it, as mentioned earlier, over a dozen times, invariably placing it at the climactic point in a sentence (a feature obscured by most of our English translations). So, literally, the sentence in verses 8–9 reads, 'Now we do not yet see all things subjected to him, but the one having been made a little lower than the angels we do see, *Jesus* . . .' For the preacher, this name sums up the full humanity of the Son of God, with all its implications. It also brings into focus a beloved person, with and through whom we can enter the presence of God and realize the destiny God intended for us. Even more wonderfully, this person, though fully acquainted with human experience, is the very self-expression of God (*cf* 1:1–4). Seeing Jesus means looking into God's life. Hebrews is deeply concerned to leave his audience in no doubt of that.

What this implies about God is both staggering and life-transforming, and needs to be absorbed by contemplation, by 'seeing', in the sense of both prayer and thought. (These two can, of course, go together, as they do so evidently and fruitfully in the work of Hebrews.) Nonetheless, what Jesus opens up about God needs to descend from our heads down into our hearts, into the innermost core of our lives, infusing our wills as well as our emotions.

The God who speaks in human terms in a Son who is Jesus does so because he has great plans for his human creatures. According to Hebrews, these plans can be discerned in the verses from Psalm 8 which he quotes in this section (2:6–8). Not that he is concerned to identify his source in the Jewish scriptures. Typically, it is enough for him that they are authoritative testimony to the purposes of God. In fact, for the most part, when he incorporates scripture passages, he presents them as spoken (rather than written) by God, Christ or the Holy Spirit (eg v6). They are God's direct communication for the present as well as the past, illuminating the significance of Jesus and the character of new covenant life.

In all probability, Psalm 8 would already have been familiar to the Hebrews community, both from their Jewish background and in relation to their Christian faith. The psalm celebrates the glory of God the creator, recognizes the littleness of humanity in relation to the vastness of the universe, and wonders at the God-given vocation of human beings to have dominion over God's creation, even in its entirety ('all things'). It takes up the theme of Genesis 1:26–31 and the role of primal Adam in Genesis 2. In early Christian thinking (and worship?), the sixth verse of the psalm seems to have become particularly associated with Christ as sovereign Lord (eg 1 Corinthians 15:27;

Ephesians 1:22; 1 Peter 3:22). Not surprisingly, because of the theme of 'subjection', it is also linked by New Testament writers with the use of Psalm 110:1 in relation to Jesus.

True to form, Hebrews refers to more of the psalm than other New Testament writers (he is given to quite lengthy quotations). He uses three verses (Psalm 8:4–6) to bring together powerfully the destiny of humankind and the person and experience of Jesus. If at this point the congregation was expecting the usual stress on the majesty and exaltation of Christ they were in for something of a shock. The preacher is about to bring them down to earth with a vengeance.

At the beginning of this section, Hebrews has talked about 'the world to come'. By this he means not a faraway heaven but a new creation, in which things are made as they were meant to be (*cf* eg Romans 8:19–23). Just as the first creation came through God's word (Genesis 1), so what God speaks in his Son makes all things new. The 'great salvation' offered by God, the new covenant with all its possibilities, inaugurates a new world order in which God's original plans will be wholly fulfilled. Humankind, in a special relationship with God, will have the great honour of being responsible for the world in a God-like way.

But that is not yet seen to have happened (2:8c). Though the way has been opened up, we are still not ready to enjoy fully the kind of caring dominion exercised by God. There is one who has made that journey, who comes from the heart of God covered in glory and honour – Jesus. Yet how did he arrive at his destination, and from where did he set out?

As the author of the Fourth Gospel would put it, Jesus

came from God and was going to God (John 13:3). As Hebrews will soon make very clear, the route required God's eternal Son to become the new Adam; to enter completely into the human experience, thereby demonstrating what human life could and should be. As representative and perfect human being, 'son of man', and as the expression of God, Jesus fleshes out God's gracious purposes as set out in Psalm 8. It cost him dearly. It meant that 'for a little while' he suffered drastic loss of 'status'. Here is a contrast with the position of humankind as presented in Psalm 8. For human beings to be only a little lower than the angels was privilege indeed. God's Son, however, was inherently superior to those spiritual beings who properly owed him worship (so Hebrews has just majestically reminded his congregation). It was quite a come-down. Yet (as 10:5–10 underlines) Jesus humbled himself willingly, for the sake of wayward and fearful humanity. It seems characteristic of the God of Jesus Christ that the welfare of those he has made means far more than any divine self-interest. God does what has to be done, whatever the consequence for his reputation.

Loss of rank, however, is not the only thing God's Son has to contend with. Becoming human means taking on the negative as well as the positive, facing and feeling the hurt of the world's dis-ease and sin. And inescapably it means going through the disintegration of death. In the case of Jesus, this experience was particularly horrific. But through it all he stayed true to his mission: to make it possible, by the grace of God, for human beings to come into their own.

About this, Hebrews has much to say. With the congregation still digesting the claim that the kingly glory of Jesus is because of, not in spite of, the suffering of death, the preacher goes on to draw out its implications. The sovereign Lord to whom they owe reverence and allegiance is to be accorded highest honour because he was willing to be totally vulnerable. It is in suffering and death that Jesus is to be perceived as King of creation. This is a hard message particularly if, in dire straits yourself, you are looking for a dramatic deliverance out of difficult circumstances by someone who is supposed to have enormous power.

Is this a recipe for despair? Hebrews is passionately concerned to get across to his community that, in fact, the reverse is the case. The reason that Jesus went through hell is so that he could be on the inside of people's problems. He knows what life can be like. And he *can* bring mighty help, help that will reach to the heart of the matter and bring salvation in its most comprehensive sense. In this context, human notions of power have to be radically reinterpreted.

In dying, Jesus entered into a universal human experience. But Hebrews stresses that, through tasting death, Jesus did 'on behalf of everyone' (2:9) what no other human being could do – he broke the stranglehold of sin and the devil, the entail of Adam's failure. Of that liberation everyone needs both to hear and to 'taste'.

Divine pioneer

What God did in Jesus was very much in character. 'It was fitting' (v10). It is clear from the Jewish scriptures that God is given to identifying and suffering with his people even as he brings them saving help. He feels their pain (Isaiah 63:9). Their condition matters to him, and he shows it. He is no remote and detached deity. Indeed, sometimes the heat of his passion becomes unbearable (as Hebrews recognizes). But the strength of divine feelings is fuelled by love and commitment. As Hosea perceived at great personal cost, despite all the provocation and rejection God receives, he will not come to destroy (Hosea 11:9). God's bias is towards deliverance. Even through the catastrophe of the Flood, it seems he could not bring himself to make a full end of the humanity he had so carefully created (Genesis 6–8). The core truth is neatly summed up in the Lord's words to Moses, in Exodus 3:7–8: 'I have indeed seen the misery of my people in Egypt. I have heard them crying out because of their slave drivers, and I am concerned about their suffering. So I have come down to rescue them from the hand of the Egyptians and to bring them up out of that land into a good and spacious land, a land flowing with milk and honey...'

Just as God launched a rescue operation to bring his afflicted people out of slavery into the Promised Land, so God acts 'in these last days' to bring many children out of bondage into glory. But this divine mission is unprecedented in scope and operation. It involves not a chosen few in a particular geographical location, but, potentially at least, every human being. This is the sense of 'many sons' in verse 10. In Jewish thinking, 'many' often had the sense of 'all' (Isaiah 53:12; *cf* Mark 14:24). And throughout his exposition Hebrews places great stress on the comprehensive significance of Jesus. He has, after all, just underlined the truth that the death of Jesus was 'for everyone' (2:9). It is as well also to remind ourselves that for our preacher the term 'sons' was very much an inclusive one (a fact acknowledged by the NRSV translation as 'children'). In the culture of the time, sons had status, privileges and rights of inheritance. In the dispensation of God, all are in this condition, whatever their gender or background (Galatians 3:26–28). We are all marked out for glory. Whether we take advantage of this is in our hands.

The salvation that Hebrews is talking about is available to many more people than were involved with the Exodus. It also engages God in much more thoroughgoing direct action. Instead of working through an agent like Moses, God speaks (and therefore acts) in one who is a Son, one who bears the very stamp of his nature. In Jesus, God enters fully and directly into the human predicament, in order to redeem humanity's potential, in order to bring us into glory. This glory is associated with far more than a localized land of promise, however Utopian. It means no less than sharing in the very life of God. It means knowing God's forgiveness and help. It means experiencing new creation: being made new and therefore being fit to exercise that healthy dominion over 'all things', which God always intended. All this is 'glory'. Because of Jesus, all this is possible. We are not there yet, and the way to glory, though open, will not be easy: it follows the path that Jesus trod. However, even on the way, there will be much to enjoy as well as much to look forward to. Hebrews also wants to emphasize this in his sermon.

In verse 10 Hebrews describes Jesus as *archēgos*, a word that can be translated and understood in various ways. It can have the sense of 'author', the one responsible for something, the originator, the source (eg Acts 3:15). It can also mean 'ruler' or 'prince' (Acts 5:31) or, more generally in that connection, one who goes first, often in dangerous circumstances, a 'pioneer', a military champion, a hero. For Hebrews, all of these senses are relevant. Jesus is

God with us

both originator and leader. He is certainly the source of salvation (*cf* Hebrews 5:9, which uses a different word). He is also the courageous leader who goes on ahead to clear the way and make it safe (if still daunting!). His task involves taking on and overcoming our greatest enemy, the one who holds the power of death, the devil (2:14).

The preacher of *Hebrews* is adept at choosing words that are rich in meaning. He uses *archēgos* once more, to great effect, at 12:2 'Let us fix our eyes on Jesus, the *archēgos* and perfecter of our faith'. The impact of both these usages would be strengthened for the original recipients of *Hebrews* by the preacher's skilful application of language. On both occasions, *archēgos* is used with a word having to do with perfection and beginning with the prefix *tel-*. At root, *arch-* is associated with beginning or primacy, *tel-* with end or consummation. Such verbal signals help to stress the comprehensive completeness of God's act of salvation – from beginning to end, from source to fulfilment. As so often in *Hebrews*, the Greek phraseology and forms of expression intensify awareness of meaning. This preacher is rhetorician and poet as well as pastor and theologian. Sadly and inevitably, much is lost when he is translated.

But how are we to understand Hebrews' contention that God made the pioneer author of salvation 'perfect through suffering'? Perfect in what sense? Was Jesus not perfect from the very beginning of his mission? We must recall the preacher's conviction that Jesus is 'reliving' the experience of Adam. As representative human being, he faces all the pressures and temptations of being human. Through them all, he stays true to God. His obedience holds firm, though it is sorely tested. He learns in his own experience what it costs to remain in God's will in an unsympathetic and sinful world. Unlike Adam, he does not fail his 'Creator'. Through many trials and temptations (the word 'suffering' is actually in the plural) Jesus fulfils the purposes of God. In that sense he is made perfect. He completes his task perfectly, despite all the pressures to the contrary. We are not to think that God inflicted hardship on Jesus 'to teach him a lesson'. God is no sadist. Neither does he stand apart from what is happening. In Jesus, God is actively involved in struggling with the hard side of life. The sufferings came into being because humankind misused their God-given freedom. These sufferings are of God only in the sense that, in Jesus, God bears the brunt of them, thus taking full responsibility for the consequences of his generosity in creation.

Jesus, our brother

Already the Hebrews community has been offered a message of profound encouragement. But the one who addresses them knows only too well that this message will need repeating, expanding and interpreting. His audience will take some convincing. Their confidence is at a low ebb. They are disillusioned. Hope is in short supply. So, it seems, is their capacity to take in the nature and consequences of mature Christian faith.

The preacher of *Hebrews* is not one to shirk this challenge. Now, therefore, he spells out for his listeners an amazing truth about their relationship with Jesus (2:11–16). They are his brothers and sisters. They are from the same family (v11). They are kin. To express this solidarity with them, Jesus became flesh and blood, as they were (v14). And, despite all their weakness and sin, he is not ashamed to own them as relatives. He wants to make

God with us

them holy, certainly; but he does this by coming among them, not by dispensing orders from a distance.

Jesus is, in a supreme sense, the Son of God (1:1–4) but those created in God's image are also God's children. From the beginning, there has been a vital connection between God and humankind. In the humanity of Jesus, this connection is given flesh, showing us that, like Jesus, we can be at home with God. Though we are not of God in the same way as the eternal Son, our origin and destiny are nonetheless in God. With God we belong. That is why God goes to so much trouble to bring us back from sin and despair. He wants our company – and our fulfilment.

This God is something to shout about! One important way of doing this is in the context of worship. There, too, says Hebrews, Jesus is right in the middle of things (2:12). Here is a timely reminder for a dispirited congregation. Jesus is not exalted out of reach. He is present with his brothers and sisters, joining them in praising (literally 'hymning') God and proclaiming to them the truth about God ('name' in verse 12 means nature and character). So Jesus is involved in liturgy and teaching. Such activities are part of the expression of that priestly vocation Hebrews is shortly to explore; but we notice that these activities are exercised from a position 'in the midst' of the congregation. There is no standing on ceremony nor stress on separation. That perhaps is a lesson in itself for God's people and their leaders. It is a lesson reinforced when we ponder also on those other occasions in the New Testament where Jesus is described as being 'in the middle' (*cf* Matthew 18:20; Luke 24:36; John 19:18; 20:19).

Precisely how Jesus operates within the assembly Hebrews does not elaborate. One thing he may well have had in mind is the proclamation of scripture. We have seen

53

how he regards words from scripture as words spoken directly by God, Jesus or the Spirit. So here, Jesus is presented as speaking the words of Psalm 22:22 – words of praise and adoration, perhaps also of prophecy and exhortation.

The Hebrews community were no doubt assembled for worship when they heard Hebrews' 'word of exhortation'. It is in that setting that the preacher is trying to put fresh heart into them. Despite their unhappy (and unexpectant?) condition, Jesus is with them – just as he is with them at every moment and in every aspect of their lives. He can even deliver them from the primal fear of death through which the devil holds them in thrall. For them, such fear might have a particular potency because of the threat of persecution. Hebrews is careful not to say that they will escape death. This is an experience which must still be passed through. But he confidently asserts that through Jesus it has been robbed of its power to dominate and overshadow life. Because of the victory of Jesus, they are freed to realize that death can lead to glory. Therefore life can be lived to the full. The challenge before them is like that which faced Jesus: to put their trust in God (2:13) and not be dragged down by the depressing legacy of a defeated devil.

Jesus, the high priest

At the climax of his overture, Hebrews now makes explicit a theme which is of crucial importance to his message. He wants to share his vision of Jesus as high priest (vv17–18). He knows that in their present state the Hebrews community will find this understanding of Jesus difficult to grasp (*cf* 5:11). He is also sure that taking it in could make all the difference to their future pilgrimage. He therefore prepares the way carefully in his opening exposition and he unfolds his vision in stages through the rest of his sermon. Skilled preacher that he is, he does not ask his congregation to cope with the full picture all at once.

The priestly character of Jesus has already been hinted at. Now it is brought clearly into focus. And all that Hebrews has said so far must be borne in mind, if this first real sight of the picture is to be understood aright. The Jesus who is high priest is the one so strikingly portrayed as Son of God and representative new Adam.

As Jewish listeners would be well aware, it was the high priest who once a year had the terrifying responsibility of entering the Most Holy Place, that innermost shrine of the Tabernacle or Temple where the presence of God was believed specially to dwell. He entered with great caution, having undergone stringent rites of purification. Carrying sacrificial animal blood, he sought to make atonement for the sins of the people, to make right their relationship with God (Leviticus 16). He went as the people's representative, healthily aware of the overwhelming holiness of God. This is an image Hebrews will make more of later (especially in chapter 9), when he will emphasize that such a ceremony can get nowhere near the heart of the matter. The ritual was God-given and served an important human need; but it had been rendered obsolete by the 'real thing'. Because of Jesus, it was no longer necessary. Jesus is the perfect self-expression of God (1:1–14) *and* the perfect expression of humanity, as God intended it to be (2:6–10). Jesus therefore, and he alone, can perfectly fulfil the priestly vocation of bringing together for good a holy God and a sinful people. He does this, not with ritual caution but with wholehearted involvement – and at the cost of his life. Even more awesome, when we look at Jesus we see into the true character of God. It is no less than the holy God himself who is making full and decisive atonement for the sins of the people. We have a priestly God.

This is underlined by the description of Jesus the high priest as 'merciful and faithful'. These adjectives are never used in the Old Testament in relation to the high priest. They *are* used frequently of God. God's mercy and faithfulness are inherent in the priesthood he expresses in Jesus. Divine faithfulness means that this high priest can be utterly depended upon. He will never fail or forsake his people whatever the circumstances. Divine mercy means something much more than the setting aside of wrath or punishment. It is a quality of exquisite tenderness born of understanding love. This priest feels for us and with us. And this priest, as no other, can bring us mighty help in our times of testing suffering.

His overture completed, Hebrews now goes on to draw out its main themes: the primacy and character of God; the nature and significance of Jesus as divine and human; the high priestly work of God in Jesus; the imperative of steadfast commitment to a new covenant. Together, these make powerful music, music that can minister profoundly to every condition. All we need are ears to hear and hearts to respond.

4

GOD OF TRUTH AND PROMISE

Hebrews 3:1 – 6:20

Jesus, the head of God's household

All that has been said so far should have encouraged the congregation to fix their thoughts on Jesus. Hebrews wants to keep attention focussed on him, for he is the way in to the presence of God. No human leader, however gifted or significant, can or should take the place of Jesus. The preacher has already stressed that Jesus is greater than the angels. He is certainly superior to the most significant earthly figures in the tradition of the people of God. Hebrews now insists that even the revered Moses was but God's faithful servant. Jesus is God's faithful Son. He is also God's 'apostle' (3:1). This is the only place in the New Testament where Jesus is so described, though there are many references elsewhere (especially in the Fourth Gospel) to Jesus being 'sent' (the basic meaning of 'apostle'). For Hebrews, Jesus was sent by God on a special and unique mission to set people free, and to set them free in a far more wonderful and extensive sense than in the Exodus mission of Moses. The deliverance Jesus wins is comprehensive. It covers every aspect of life. It leads to a promised land – heaven. When there is Jesus to look to, why fix attention on anyone else? Jesus is the only one who brings people directly into the liberating heart of God.

Encounter with God in Hebrews

The 'house' spoken of here is primarily the household or people of God (3:3–6). In this connection, Hebrews takes up another theme he has introduced earlier. God's people, as brothers and sisters of Jesus (2:10–13), are called to be members of God's family. Their vocation is 'heavenly' (3:1). Their home is with God, and their household is overseen by the one who is at the same time God's faithful and merciful Son and their deeply understanding brother (2:11–18). He is also their priest, that 'great priest over the house of God' (10:21) who gives them confidence to draw near to the God who loves them. What more could they want?

Yet then, as now, there are forces and pressures that work to break up God's family, to set us at odds with one another or to drive some to leave home (*cf* 10:25). Family disagreements can be among the most bitter and long-lasting of conflicts and the enemy is poised to take full advantage of this unhappy state of affairs. So we need plentiful supplies of courage and hope. And we need the perseverance to hold on to them (3:6), especially when life in God's household feels to be more trouble than it is worth. Endurance was evidently a much undervalued quality in the Hebrews community (and still is in many of its modern counterparts). Hebrews will return to the vital importance of endurance again and again.

He will also come back to the word translated by the NIV as 'courage' – *parrēsia*. Here is another term which carries a wealth of meaning (amply borne out by the range of translations in our English versions). It is a very active, up-front kind of word. It has the sense of boldness, of confidence, of total frankness and honesty, of freedom of speech. For Hebrews, it is just the sort of word that he needs to express the character of a believer's relationship with God and consequent approach to life. There fear, reticence, inhibition and pretence are unnecessary, out of place. When we know the truth of God's attitude towards us, we can be bold indeed, whatever our circumstances.

How do we know that truth? He will do more spelling out later, but the preacher has already pointed us firmly in the right direction. That direction is Jesus.

Responding to God

The God who is more than worthy of confidence is profoundly hurt and angered when his beloved people turn against him and away from him. As Hebrews perceives it, it is crucial to remember that in no sense do we have an unfeeling God. By our response to God's costly love, we can either delight his heart, or break it. The preacher of *Hebrews* makes this very clear (3:7-19).

In his comparison between Jesus and Moses, he now recalls what happened after the Exodus, during the critical time the people of God spent in the wilderness. It is a story with which his audience would be thoroughly familiar – perhaps too familiar to see easily the serious challenge it posed for them. In a real and dangerous sense, the Hebrews community were going through a new wilderness experience, having experienced a 'great salvation'. They should learn – and learn quickly – from the mistakes of their forebears.

Using Psalm 95, Hebrews points graphically to the effects of the Israelites' disobedience, rebellion and lack of trust. Despite being liberated from crushing slavery by the mighty work of God, they quickly became discontented. Their memories were short. Thankfulness soon evaporated. When the going became hard, so did their hearts.

Thus they closed themselves off from that fulness of life (God's 'rest') which God had lovingly been planning for them. It is small wonder that this caused God anguish. In our flawed human condition, we know the power and the pain of those feelings aroused when costly love is rejected. God suffers them in all the purity of love's perfection.

Hebrews emphasizes that a vital and effective way of guarding against the development of rebellious hardness of heart is mutual encouragement among the people of God (3:12–13). God's people need each other. God's people need to recall to one another the saving faithfulness of God, to bear one another up when times are testing. God's people are called to stand together, not in complaining disobedience but in persevering trust. And God's people are to take advantage of the present moment. They must respond to God's prompting 'as long as it is called Today' (v13). The time to trust God and to encourage sisters and brothers is *now*. It will not do to put off response until 'tomorrow'. The old saying, 'Tomorrow never comes', is true.

One thing God's people can help each other to realize is how deceitful is sin (v13). Sin is a trickster, obscuring the real truth of a matter. It skews perspectives, pulling our eyes away from looking to Jesus. It causes people to turn their backs on the one relationship that can bring their lives to fulfilment – a relationship with the living God (v12). For Hebrews, sin is essentially the betrayal of this relationship; it is being unfaithful to God. It goes far deeper than the breaking of rules. It is the rejection of a Person. It is a profound breach of trust. Yet, as Hebrews will later stress, sin will be met with forgiveness for those who so desire it. Hurt God may be (and his anguish is not to be taken lightly), but the desire of *his* heart is for a heart-to-heart relationship with people. He will go to any lengths to make that possible. That is what the new covenant is about.

In trying to open his hearers' eyes to the real nature and serious consequences of the sin of unfaithfulness, Hebrews again underlines the importance of determined perseverance (v14). Though the honeymoon period may be over, the reason for their confidence in the relationship is just as well-founded in the time of testing as it was in the euphoria of beginning. If they can only believe it, they will not be disappointed in their hope.

The best is yet to be

God longs for his people to enter into his divine Sabbath-rest (4:1). That rest marks the fulfilment of creative activity and rejoicing in a job well done (*cf* Genesis 2:2–3). With this delightful prospect before them, the recipients of *Hebrews* are further challenged. Though this 'rest' is entirely God's gift, it does require effort on their part to take advantage of it (4:11). Like the Israelites of old, they need to hear God's good news of liberation and life. They need to hear God's voice – a voice which is most clearly articulated in Jesus. But hearing is not enough. They need to accept, to respond in faith to the truth of what they hear. And they need to continue in persevering trust even when it feels as if God has abandoned them in the barren wilderness.

Such perseverance can be very hard work. It is not easy to keep going when God seems far away or even to have turned against us. Yet it is hard work that God crowns with rest – and not just after the end of our earthly lives. Enjoying the blessings of God's presence is something for here and now, whatever our worldly circumstance (vv3, 11). We can enter God's rest in a way that the ancient Israelites never could. After their extended and rebellious time in the wilderness, Joshua ('Jesus' in Greek) led them, with some difficulty, into the Promised Land (v8). The greater Joshua, Jesus the Son of God, leads us into the glory of heaven. And we can enter that glory, that vibrant rest, today – and every day.

Throughout the section from 3:7 to 4:11, and using Psalm 95 as a focus, Hebrews has been interweaving the themes of Exodus and Creation (*cf* the latter part of the book of *Isaiah*, eg 51:9–16). It is a telling juxtaposition. For both prophet and psalmist, the mighty deliverance of God is akin to a new act of creation. It brings a momentous new beginning. How much more the great salvation through which God brings humanity into its destined glory! Just as Paul perceived that those who are in Christ are a new creation (2 Corinthians 5:17), so Hebrews, in a more extended exposition, sees the work of God in saving us as bringing forth a new world – a new age in its truest sense (Hebrews 1:1; 2:5–10). There is much to be done if we are to grow into maturity in this new context (5:11–14). However, a 'birth' has happened. The image of God's salvation as 'birthing' is particularly important in the Johannine tradition (eg John 1:10–13; 3:1–15) but it is also an underlying thought in *Hebrews*. So the verb 'to bring into' (2:10) even then had connotations of giving birth, as well as being used frequently in the Pentateuch of God bringing his people into the Promised Land. For Hebrews, here again is a fruitful fusion of the motifs of deliverance and creation. And here again is his facility to choose words which, in their richness of meaning, open up trains of thought rather than closing off possibilities.

Indeed, the diet is *so* rich that we can well imagine the congregation protesting that they would need more time to digest it properly! Here is a sermon that needs some pondering.

The naked truth

Hebrews' words also beg for an active response. The section that we now arrive at (4:12–16) is certainly a case in point. First, he bids his hearers recall the stark reality of their position before God. He does so in language which continues the creation theme by alluding to the experience of the first Adam (*cf* Genesis 3:24).

The Sabbath-rest into which Christians should strive to enter (Hebrews 4:11) is an experience denied to the Israelites in the desert because of their disobedience and lack of trust. These sins were at the heart of Adam's failure – that fallen Adam who tried to hide himself from God but whose nakedness was revealed by the divine word (Genesis 3:8–12). God's searching voice exposed him completely, both outwardly and inwardly. So it is with Adam's descendants. We are utterly laid bare before the God who made us. We can cover up nothing, including those aspects of our being that we are reluctant to admit – even to ourselves. We are totally open and accountable to the God whose penetrating word pierces to the heart of our vulnerable nakedness. When the truth of this hits us, it is frightening. What will God's response be? Will this God come to destroy? In our thoroughly unprotected condition, the kind of God before whom we are exposed will make all the difference in the world. Adam discovered that though he was under judgement, God still cared for him. God made clothes for him and his partner (Genesis 3:21).

What of us?

Having made his community face the core truth about themselves, Hebrews continues immediately with a message of encouragement (Hebrews 4:14ff). He exposes the fundamental truth about God. As a preacher who passionately cares for his congregation, he wants to lead them into real hope, not push them further into despair.

If we are laid bare before God, says Hebrews, then God lays himself bare before us. God's response to our inherent weakness and failure is not to condemn or destroy but, in Jesus, to experience for himself what it means to be human in a fallen world.

It is at this point in his exposition that Hebrews returns to speaking of Jesus as high priest. He again makes it clear (*cf* 2:17–18) that this high priest is fully representative of our human condition. As the new Adam, Jesus has confronted the full force of temptation. Though he resisted, he knows only too well what it feels like to be tempted and so can identify with us in our struggles (4:15). Jesus is also fully representative of God. He is the Son of God (v14) in the supreme way underlined by the preacher at the outset of his sermon. So, in the most literal sense, 'God knows'. God knows the truth of our condition, and not just from a holy distance. God has inside knowledge.

This is priesthood *par excellence*. It means that all can approach God's presence with *parrēsia* – with boldness and confidence, in total honesty and frankness and with the privilege of freedom of speech – sure of an understanding and loving welcome. Though we cannot hide from God, we can trust him to understand our condition and to bring us the saving help we so much need. Before this God, grovelling fear is totally inappropriate. At the throne of grace there is mercy in abundance from a God who wants us to be with him. We should therefore make full use of the privilege opened up to us by our great high priest, that of continually and boldly drawing near to the presence of God. Here, and whenever we choose, we can enter into God's 'rest'.

Our priestly Jesus, the Son of God, makes it clear that we can enter into God's presence directly. We do not need an intermediary, a specially appointed holy person to do it on our behalf. The priestly God has demonstrated that the door is open, and that he freely invites us in.

The extent of God's priestly love

Not surprisingly, Hebrews compares Jesus more than favourably with the high priests of the Jewish tradition. As Jesus is greater than the angels, greater than Moses, greater than Joshua, so, it should already be evident, is he greater than the priests of Aaron's line.

The comparison is (typically) very carefully structured. It is almost a mini-sermon! Three points about 'every high priest' (5:1–4) are related to Jesus in reverse order (vv5–10), so giving a pattern of *a b c c b a*. The use of the term 'high priest' in verses 1 and 10 binds the section together though, as a result of the intervening discussion, the term has a rather different sense at the end than at the beginning. Seeing Jesus as high priest requires seeing priesthood in a new way.

The three points have to do with salvation from sin (a), compassionate weakness (b) and divine vocation (c). All these aspects of priestly ministry, argues the preacher, Jesus demonstrates to perfection. Priesthood is not a matter of one's choosing. It is God's gift, God's vocation (c). Like Aaron before him, Jesus is certainly called by God – and in a unique sense (vv4–6). As eternal Son of God, his vocation is to express fully God's longing that all humanity should share the divine glory. Because of who he is, Jesus the high priest can also offer a salvation (a) which is totally and eternally effective (vv1,9). No Jewish high priest, though called by God, could achieve such results.

The remaining point under discussion (vv2,3,7,8 – point b) is of great interest. Verse 2 is, in fact, an extraordinary statement, for nowhere in the Old Testament are pastoral sympathy and gentle care presented as a feature of priesthood (cultic sacrifice, teaching and leading are, rather, the major emphases). Hebrews' view here seems to be coloured by his experience of Christ who in the days of his life on earth 'offered up prayers and petitions with loud cries and tears to the one who could save him from death, and he was heard for his reverent submission' (v 7). Here is a graphic illustration of that complete identification with the human condition already highlighted by the preacher when speaking of Jesus, Son of God and high priest. 'Loud cries and tears' – and on his own behalf (a reference, perhaps, to Gethsemane). Faced with the prospect, and the fear, of grim death, Jesus cried out with great wrenching sobs for God to save him. He did not relish suffering and death. The prospect appalled him.

Here also is the living pattern for that bold honesty with which we are urged to approach the throne of grace. The Son of God knew weakness, fear and anguish from the inside and he did not hesitate to express in prayer just how he felt. His agonized prayer is described as 'reverent submission'. The same term is used in 12:28, where Christians are exhorted to offer to God acceptable worship with 'reverence and awe'. What a liberating understanding of reverence – coming before God just as you are and telling

God of truth and promise

it just how it is! This is a tremendous encouragement. True reverence involves personal honesty, not pious pretence. Through the priestly example and ministry of Jesus, God sets us free to be who we really are.

Note that the preacher says that the desperate prayer of Jesus was 'heard'. But he was not saved *from* death. He still had to confront that terror. The salvation came *out of* death: God granted Jesus the power to endure, and brought from the horror an outcome of new life and joy (*cf* 12:2).

The Hebrews congregation has already been given a great deal to chew on. There is more. At verse 6, and again in verse 10, the preacher introduces an ingredient of Jesus' priesthood that is going to be very difficult to take in. Quoting Psalm 110:4 (the only New Testament writer to do so), he asserts that God had designated Jesus 'a priest for ever, in the order of Melchizedek'. Hebrews has much to explain about this. In his judgement, however, the community is not quite ready to receive his message. He needs to do a little more preparation.

Grow up!

The writer of *Hebrews* is clearly very disappointed in the Christians he is addressing! By now they should have grown up into mature faith. Instead, they have stayed at the baby stage (5:11–12). Infantile faith can indeed be a very tempting proposition long after it has ceased to be appropriate. Dependency, being cared for rather than taking responsibility, enjoying food that slips down easily without making too many demands on the digestive system – such comforting and self-centred security has its attractions. Yet when succumbed to, the temptations of inappropriate babyhood seriously retard spiritual growth (v13), not only of the individuals concerned but also of the church to which they belong. This leads to the loss of much creative opportunity to explore and communicate the deep things of God (*cf* 5:14 – 6:1–3).

The immature Christians of *Hebrews* are severely warned of a further danger of their condition – the possibility of falling away from faith completely (6:4–8). To the preacher this is a matter of the utmost urgency and gravity. If they receive all the tremendous blessings of salvation and new covenant life and then knowingly turn their backs on them, it would be tantamount to crucifying the Son of God again and bringing him into public contempt. Restoring such people to repentance is well nigh impossible because they are steadfastly looking in the wrong direction and defying God.

However, the Hebrews community has not regressed that far. The preacher has opened up a horrifying prospect in order to shock them into persevering. He is careful, also, to assure them that God will not overlook those praiseworthy qualities they have held on to, even in this time of crisis (vv9–12). As always, God sees the whole picture.

God honours his promises

God and God's promises can be totally relied upon. Such is the truth to which Hebrews now points his wavering community (vv13–20).

The way God treated Abraham is typical of the way God deals with his people. We should find this profoundly encouraging. God made and bound himself to a solemn promise. Without denying his very nature, God could not

God of truth and promise

but honour that promise. Yet Abraham had to exercise great patience and trust before he saw the promise begin to be fulfilled in the birth of Isaac. And there came a time when even that precarious beginning seemed to be in jeopardy. Further, the promise was not wholly realized until long after Abraham's lifetime.

We, too, can be confident in exercising this kind of persevering trust because it is the same God of Abraham who makes a promise to us – that, as forgiven sinners, we can share God's life. This we can hold on to as a sure and certain hope, an anchor to keep our faith steady, when pressures threaten us and God *seems* far away. It may well be that our faith is sorely tested, but the reality is always that God will never go back on his word.

Right at the end of the passage (6:19b,20), the imagery changes, though not the message. Now the picture is of the Holy of Holies, that most sacred place in the Tabernacle (or Temple) where God's Presence was believed to dwell. Only the High Priest was allowed in, once a year on the Day of Atonement. As the people's holy representative, and carrying sacrificial animal blood, he sought God's cleansing for the sins of the community under the old covenant. So Hebrews returns to the theme that plays such an important part in his exposition – the high priesthood of Jesus. After careful preparing of the ground we are about to be made aware of just how shockingly radical the priesthood of Jesus really is.

5

GOD OF NEW BEGINNINGS

Hebrews 7 – 10

The order of Melchizedek

Earlier (5:6,10), the writer of *Hebrews* has told his community that the priesthood of Jesus is 'in the order of Melchizedek'. Now the time has come to try to spell out what that means (7:1–10). For Hebrews, seeing Jesus as great high priest opened up much of God's truth. It highlighted the wonder and extent of God's gracious dealings with humanity. Yet in human terms and according to Jewish Law, Jesus was not qualified to be a priest (vv13–14). He did not come from the priestly tribe of Levi. Like the Davidic kings before him, he came from the tribe of Judah. Here was a real problem for the preacher, convinced as he surely was that his vision of the priesthood of Jesus came from God.

Very probably, the way through came for the writer when he pondered on Psalm 110:4. (Psalm 110:1 was clearly a popular text in the New Testament Church, but Hebrews is the only one to use verse 4.) Its hint of an eternal priesthood in the order of Melchizedek pointed him back to Genesis 14, the only other place in the Old Testament where this mysterious figure is mentioned. Here was a priest, greatly honoured by God, who was not a member of the tribe of Levi nor even of the chosen race.

He was an unqualified outsider who played an extremely marginal part in old covenant history. There is (fragmentary) evidence, from the Dead Sea Scrolls and more clearly from Jewish literature which post-dates the New Testament, that Melchizedek came to be regarded by some as a heavenly, angelic figure involved in spiritual warfare. But there is no indication from the text of *Hebrews* that its author had in mind any such notion. It is the scriptural material which forms the focus of his pondering. Using a technical form of argument common in Judaism, Hebrews concludes from his meditation that the outsider Melchizedek, king and priest, was greater than Abraham or Levi. His priesthood was of a different and superior order. There is no mention in the Old Testament of Melchizedek's genealogical background. For a Jewish priest (who must prove his legitimacy by reference to genealogy) this would be an unthinkable omission. In Melchizedek's case, Hebrews argues, it points to the *permanence* of his priesthood. It is without beginning or end.

In this (and in his messianic qualities of righteousness and peace), Melchizedek resembles the priestly Son of God. Jesus is, of course, far greater than Melchizedek. Hebrews is careful to stress that Melchizedek has been made like the Son of God; the Son of God has not been made like Melchizedek (7:3). But it is this strange king's sort of priesthood that Jesus expresses to perfection.

God is full of surprises! For Jewish listeners, all this really would have been quite revolutionary. It is not without its lessons for us.

God as 'law-breaker'!

One of those lessons is that we cannot pin God down –

even to the rules of his own making. We must always allow for the often disturbing fact that God can and does do new things. He certainly did with regard to the priesthood of Jesus. When God expressed his own priestly nature in his Son, he broke with his own tradition; he broke with the law he himself had given. To understand the priesthood of God's Son, we have to look behind and beyond the established system.

The weakness, sin and mortality of the priests of Aaron's line meant that they could never fully break down the barrier between sinful humanity and God. God's unexpected solution to this problem was to make regulations concerning ancestry irrelevant (though, in fact, no-one could claim a more impeccable genealogy than Jesus the Son of God!) As far as God was concerned, what was important was the inherent character of the priest and the effectiveness of his priestly ministry. This meant far more than conformity to established rules.

Jesus conquered death and lives for ever. Jesus is the holy self-expression of God. Jesus can do what the law, infected with human weakness, can never do; that is, bring us into a new and saving relationship with God for ever. Thus our salvation is guaranteed – and by the highest authority.

Jesus, the divinely appointed priest in the order of Melchizedek (5:5,10; 7:17,21) is also God's Son, the perfect expression of God's being and will (1:1–3). He thus receives his priesthood directly from God, a priesthood which fully expresses God's own priestly character and ministry. It therefore scatters all shadows, is complete in itself and eternal in efficacy. It needs no successors. As 7:24 makes clear, this priesthood is 'intransmissible' (the literal sense of the word translated 'permanent' in NIV).

It cannot be passed on because Jesus lives for ever and has decisively fulfilled the fundamental priestly vocation of bringing humanity and God together for good. There is no further need for a priestly order handed on from generation to generation. That has served its purpose and its inadequacies are manifest (7:11,18,19,27,28).

If the Hebrews community is being tempted back into the old order, the preacher is doing his very best to convince his listeners that this would be folly. It is the priestly ministry of Jesus, with its outcome of eternal salvation, which should enable them to face life with confidence, even during trying times. It should give them a much 'better hope' (v19) than the former system. They have the very oath of God as their assurance of that, an oath all the more binding in Hebrews' view because it comes later than the giving of the ritual law and therefore supersedes it (v28).

There is one aspect of the priesthood of Jesus which should give them (and us) particular encouragement. As Hebrews puts it, 'Therefore he is able to save completely those who come to God through him, because he always lives to intercede for them' (v25). Believers are constantly being held in prayer at the loving heart of God. It is important to grasp the sense of the verb 'intercede' here. It does not mean that Jesus has to plead with God to help us. God does not need convincing either that we need his mercy and grace or that he ought to dispense them. We have been reminded by Hebrews in no uncertain terms that it is God who has always taken the initiative in reaching out to his people. His mercy and grace have always been operative and he exercises them to perfection in his Son. He needs no persuading to care for his people. No 'special pleading' is required. The relationship between

God and his Son is one of utter unity. They are at one, not least in the great enterprise of redemption (1:1–3; 10:7,9). So the Son's prayer is God's own prayer.

The substance of this prayer is that, through Jesus, our lives and circumstances are taken directly into the life of God. Everything about us is known to God and matters to God. And, whether or not we realise it, God is actively involved for good in every area of our lives. The prayer of God, like his word, will not return to him empty.

We must also remember that Jesus the high priest does not, like the high priests of old, go into the presence of God *instead* of us. He invites us to go *with* him, to have our own prayer conversation with God at the throne of grace. There, as Hebrews has so graphically emphasized earlier in his sermon, we can simply and boldly be ourselves before the God who has our best interests at heart.

As we ponder the significance and wonder of the prayer of Jesus, the priestly Son of God, it would be fruitful to look also at Romans 8. Here (Romans 8:26,27,34) Paul speaks of both the Spirit and Christ Jesus as intercessors with the God who is 'for us' and from whose love nothing can separate us.

In the order of – but greater than – Melchizedek

By the end of the section we know as chapter 7, Hebrews has hammered home his conviction that Jesus is a high priest who is very different from a high priest of the traditional Jewish order. Melchizedek can point powerfully to this difference but he cannot approach the fulness of the priesthood of the Son of God. Great though he is, he is not the Son of God (v3). Though his priesthood is permanent, he cannot offer eternal salvation. He cannot contain, or prefigure, all that needs to be said about Jesus the high priest (nothing and no one can do that). He does not live for ever to make intercession for us. He is certainly not God's final word, nor agent and sustainer of creation. He did not, in dying, defeat the power of the devil. He did not learn obedience through what he suffered. He did not sacrifice his own life in order to release all the blessings of the new covenant and open the way to glory.

This last point draws our attention to a truth that is so amazing it is almost beyond words. It has been implicit throughout the sermon so far. At 7:27 Hebrews makes it explicit: 'he offered himself'. In Jesus, God is not only the priestly offerer; he is also the offering. The Priest is himself the Victim. God gives his life for us.

This staggering claim is explored by the preacher in chapters 8 to 10 in terms of the Jewish sacrificial cultus (in particular the ritual of the Day of Atonement) and of the inauguration of a new covenant. The imagery would certainly have hit home to the Hebrews community. It may not be so immediately meaningful to us. But it would do us a power of good to persevere in teasing out its fundamental and changeless truth.

Away with shadows!

Jesus, our great high priest, is the 'real thing'. The preacher's concern to emphasize this cause for celebration leads him to make comparisons with the past (8:1–6).

The priests and the centre of worship provided under the old covenant law were but a 'copy and shadow' of God's truth. The God-given ritual law sketched an 'outline impression' of divine holiness and God's desire to have fellowship with his people. But shadows do not give a complete picture of whatever casts them. They can indeed mislead and distort because of our inadequate perception. So with the law, put into operation by imperfect human beings whose vision was at best blurred. As a result, the dominant message conveyed was of the unapproachableness of God and the despairing impossibility of being holy enough to come into his presence.

Clearly God needed to expose the whole truth: that the desire of his heart and the substance of his promise was to share with humanity his forgiveness and his life. This truth he expressed by establishing a new and better (ie complete) covenant, one which revealed the full extent of his love, one which opened people's eyes to the reality of heaven.

More than anything else, people needed to 'see Jesus', the one in whom God's truth becomes apparent, full-blooded and accessible. Looking to Jesus makes it folly to lurk in the shadows, however fascinating they might appear. It can be salutary to remind ourselves of this when we are tempted to invest particular forms of worship or particular styles of leadership with exclusive divine approval. Only the worship of heaven is free of shadows. And we can join that worship, whatever earthly form we use, when we focus on Jesus, the radiance of God's glory (1:3), to whom, alone among leaders, we owe absolute allegiance.

God's new covenant

God's new covenant shows up the shortcomings of the old and renders it obsolete (8:7–13).

Already, through the prophet Jeremiah, God had

pointed his people to a time when their relationship with him would be transformed (Jeremiah 31:31–34). Hebrews quotes this prophetic promise at length because he wants to underline the wonder of its fulfilment.

The old covenant had failed because of the faithlessness of God's people. What is so different about the new? The old had been based on external rules and regulations. The new covenant offers an intimate personal relationship with God. In the Bible, the verb 'to know' invariably has to do with heart knowledge rather than head knowledge. It describes the 'knowing' of close personal communion. So in the new covenant, God takes the initiative to make it possible for human beings to share *his* life, to 'know' him from the inside just as, in Jesus, God shares *our* human life from the inside. God knows. And God longs for us to know him in response.

The new covenant opens up the possibility of mutual in-depth understanding. On our part, there can be a direct relationship with God that needs no intermediaries; a relationship in which, incredibly, God both forgives and forgets. It is a relationship designed to change us for good, to build up our confidence, to encourage our faith. And it is a relationship open to us all, from the least to the greatest. In God's new covenant, all relate to God on the same terms. There can be no privileged groups with a special knowledge that brings them closer to God than those outside their circle. The humblest believer is as near to God's presence as the most brilliant theologian, or the highest of Church dignitaries, or the most charismatic of Christian leaders. The only 'qualification' needed to know the God of Jesus Christ is to have said 'Yes' to his personal invitation.

Risky blessings

Hebrews now takes some time to emphasize the superiority of the new covenant (9:1–10). He knew it was crucial that this beleaguered Jewish Christian community should get the message, for in harking back to the old covenant they were in danger of depriving themselves of God's richest blessings. There had been a certain attraction, a comfortable security, about living in accordance with external regulations and ceremonies. You knew where you were. You knew your place in the scheme of things. And there was a specialist priesthood to take the risk of dealing with God on your behalf.

The new covenant, however, was rather more challenging. It was not so much about rules and rituals as about relationship – far less defined and predictable. Now each believer had unhindered direct access to God, and that carried with it responsibility and pain as well as privilege and joy. Individuals could no longer hide behind the system and its holy leaders. They were called to enter wholeheartedly into a personal relationship with God, a relationship which would expose them utterly and yet be the making of them; a relationship rooted and grounded in God's unchangeable love, yet often unpredictable in its detail and radical in its demand. Not least, it involved a cleansing of conscience from the inside, not, as before, a salving of conscience by some outward vicarious act. Allowing God to work from within on your own personality, motivation and behaviour can hurt deeply, even as it heals.

Nonetheless, as Hebrews goes on to underline, taking full advantage of God's new covenant will be infinitely worthwhile. The effectiveness of that covenant does not depend on any external provision or circumstance. In whatever situation we find ourselves, the full resources of God are always available to us.

Worth dying for

Under the old covenant, cleansing and forgiveness were sought after by the sacrificial shedding of blood (9:13–14). Blood represented life. To offer blood was to offer life. It was a sign of the seriousness with which sin was taken, an acknowledgement that humanity had polluted the holy purposes of God. The dedicated offering of life-blood was perceived to be an appropriate way of expressing the depths of a repentance that might bring about God's cleansing renewal. But the life offered was that of an animal, something apart from human experience. It was an offering that did not necessarily reflect a change in inner attitudes but could only bring assurance of outward, ritual cleansing.

The new covenant is based on something gloriously different. There is still the offering of a life, this time a human life, the life of Jesus (vv11–12,15). Here is a life without blemish, because it is the expression in human form of the life of God. Wonderfully, God has done in Jesus what no sinful high priest could ever do: given his very life as a sign of his total love for and commitment to us. If God is willing to go this far, we can have no doubt that his forgiveness is real, penetrating and lasting.

Unlike those who first heard this striking sermon, we may find this sacrificial imagery alien (vv16–22), knowable only from reading rather than experience. But the truth behind it is as relevant as ever. God's love for us knows no limits, even when it involves the most appalling suffering. Like a devoted parent or lover, but in perfect measure, God is willing to lay down his life for those dear to him – and that means all of us. The legacy he leaves us (his covenant or will) is nothing less than deep-down forgiveness and eternal life. We could ask for no richer blessing. Yet we need to recall that it is a treasure to be shared. We are given all this not merely for selfish enjoyment but so that we may 'serve the living God', whom death could not destroy.

An unrepeatable offering

One of the key points that Hebrews wants to press home is that the saving death of Jesus was 'once for all' (9:23–28). It is unrepeatable because it has achieved its purpose absolutely and eternally. The old covenant cultus, infected with human frailty, could never bring about such finality. Christ's death has decisively offered us an effective way of release from sin and guilt. To follow that way certainly involves commitment. What it does not involve is continuing uncertainty about the reality of our acceptability to God. Neither does it involve the need to try and appease God by holy deeds and observances, or even by means of self-punishment of one sort or another. Such things are totally unnecessary, not to say spiritually unhealthy!

With the death of Christ, God has inaugurated a new order: what Hebrews calls 'these last days' (1:2) and 'the end of the ages' (9:26). It is the order of things originally planned by God for creation but ruined by human wilfulness. It involves a heart-to-heart personal and co-operative relationship between human beings and God. Such is the fulfilment, the 'end', of God's purposes. And we are offered opportunities to become part of this fulfilment; as forgiven children to enjoy the presence of God; as those on the road to glory, to undertake a demanding journey from self-centredness to God-centredness.

All this is cause for great rejoicing – even if tempered by some natural apprehension! But Hebrews reminds us that there is even more to look forward to with eager anticipation. Jesus came to die for us 'once for all' (and in verse 28 Hebrews uses language reminiscent of that used to describe the Suffering Servant of Isaiah 53). Jesus will come again a second time to claim his own and to bring God's great work of salvation to its perfect end. As another writer was to put it, 'Amen. Come, Lord Jesus' (Revelation 22:20).

The one, true sacrifice

Hebrews has no hesitation in hammering home the 'once for all' character of Christ's self-offering (Hebrews 10:1–18). The lesson of this unrepeatable event is so vital that it warrants much repeating! And it is not just the original Jewish recipients who needed convincing. Many Christians today find it difficult *really* to accept in their heart of hearts that God has done all that is necessary to forgive their sin and open up the way to heaven. It seems too good to be true. It also subtly hurts our pride, for it requires us to acknowledge that we are far from perfect and that we cannot make things right with God by our own efforts. God had to do it for us. Our part is simply, humbly and thankfully to accept a gift willingly given.

It is a gift which carried an enormous cost – and this, too, can be hard for us to bear. It does not always feel comfortable to be 'beholden' to such an extent. Yet here is the truth of the matter. Out of committed love, God in Jesus gave his life for us in a once-and-for-all act. But the consequences of that act go on for ever. Jesus poured out his life for us on the cross so that God might pour his life into us for all eternity. We shall realize and receive the transforming wonder of that as we allow ourselves to be drawn ever more deeply into personal relationship with the God of the new covenant. So we shall discover that this God neither rubs our noses in the dirt of our failure nor selfishly insists on craven expressions of gratitude. Always and for ever God has our best interests at heart.

It is at this point in his exposition that Hebrews makes clear the fundamental character of true sacrifice. External sacrifices are not the answer; we cannot in any sense buy God's favour. What delights God's heart and releases the divine purpose is the willing personal dedication to God of total obedience, co-operation and love.

As ever, Jesus shows the way (vv5–10).

Drawing near to God

The community is now urged to take full advantage of new covenant life (10:19–25). Jesus has opened the way into God's presence, not just for the chosen few but for everyone who will come. It would surely be wasted opportunity of the highest order not to draw near continually to the God who wants to love us into fulness of life! Yet, if we are honest, many of us hold back. For all kinds of reasons, we keep close personal relationship with God at arm's length. The conscious explanation we often give ourselves is lack of time. There is too much else we have to be doing. One day, when we're not quite so busy... It could be a very fruitful exercise prayerfully to explore where the barriers *really* are. If, as may well be the case, fear is involved, this passage might give us profound reassurance.

God can be trusted. God is faithful. God has done more than enough to show us that he wants our company. Certainly God also wants to do a deep work of cleansing and reformation in our lives; but he will do it in a way that is appropriate and bearable for each one of us, and it will be infinitely worthwhile. As Hebrews stresses, we can come to God with bold confidence and complete honesty, sure of a wholehearted welcome. We can be ourselves with God as with no-one else. In God's presence we are both acceptable and joyfully accepted.

Though Hebrews has said much about this in his exposition, we do not simply have to take his word. We can prove it in our own personal experience. We can be encouraged, too, by the experiences of other believers, particularly when, for us, the going is rough. Indeed, it is crucial to realize that we are not just forgiven individuals but members of a new covenant community (v25). We belong to God and therefore we belong to one another. Commitment to one another, mutual support and encouragement should not only be our duty but our joy, as we look forward together to the fulfilment of God's gracious purposes.

Another word of warning – and encouragement

The moment has come for another urgent word of warning: God's love is true love – passionately involved, not carelessly indulgent. If we deliberately spurn that love, we will inevitably incur God's righteous judgement (10:26–27). We notice, however, that Hebrews leaves the process of judgement firmly in *God's* hand (v30). God is the only one who can fully discern the truth (which is the basic meaning of judgement). God is, therefore, the only one qualified to judge. In this, most definitely, we must not presume to take God's place. Hebrews also makes it clear that the kind of offence he is warning against is deliberate rebellion against God that is persistent, wilful and extreme (vv26,29), made even worse if the sinner has formerly been willing to take advantage of the blessings of the new covenant. Hebrews is not talking about 'everyday sin'!

It is apparent that the recipients of *Hebrews* have not yet gone so far off the rails. Again (2:1–4; 6:4–8), the writer is putting before them the horror of what could happen if they walked far enough along the wrong road. He immediately follows this fearful picture with words of affirmation and encouragement (10:32–39). Remember the early days, when you joyfully endured and risked so much for God's sake. Rekindle that faith. It will be richly rewarded. The faithful God will give in full measure what he has promised. Hold on. Hold on in hope and before very long you will know the coming of God. This message echoes very clearly some of the 'crisis parables' of Jesus. Think, for example of the parable of the wise and foolish virgins (Matthew 25:1–13) or of the watchful servants (Luke 12:35–38).

'It will be good for those servants whose master finds them watching when he comes' (Luke 12:37). And God frequently comes to save at a time when we least expect him.

6

GOD OF FAITH AND COMMITMENT

Hebrews 11:1 – 13:25

What is faith?

The preacher of *Hebrews* has been urging his community to be faithful to a faithful God. But what is faith and on what is it to be based? It might be interesting to explore our own answers to these questions. Hebrews now launches on a detailed exposition of the way he sees things, calling on the witness of an impressive catalogue of people from the days of the old covenant (11:1–40).

Not all God's people had rebelled against him! Many could be looked to as great exemplars of faith. Why? Because they trusted God even when they did not see immediate results, even when they did not clearly understand. They believed God would honour his promises and they acted accordingly, even when (as in the case of Noah!) it must have seemed to others sheer foolishness.

They responded to God's stirrings. Their faith displayed two fundamental convictions: that God existed and that God wanted to be known (v6). Moreover, this God, who authoritatively brought the universe into being out of what was not visible, was utterly trustworthy, having both the will and the power to put his purposes into effect (vv1–2).

The early heroes of faith had little else to go on but their own inner responses to an unseen God. As time went on, there was the faith of others to look to for guidance and encouragement. This can be a tremendous help. But we of the new covenant have a further incalculable advantage. The unseen God has made himself known in Jesus. In Jesus, the unseen God has demonstrated to the full that he can be trusted and that he offers us immeasurable blessing. God has spoken in a Son (1:2). What God has spoken, he will never retract.

When God's Word (who effected creation) became flesh, we were given the greatest sign God could offer of his intentions towards us. This reality should stir our hearts and wills as we move along the very varied, often difficult, terrain of our journey of faith. It is heartening to recall that we do not walk alone.

Hope for the future

Faith recognizes that with God there is always something more, something better to anticipate. For the believer, it is undoubtedly true that the best is yet to come. As Hebrews points out, the great patriarchs, in their own way, had already perceived this. Abraham is a prime example (11:8–12).

In response to the prompting of God (and at an advanced age!) Abraham left behind what was familiar and embarked on a hazardous journey into the unknown. He trusted God's amazing promise of descendants and land, even though he knew he would not live to see its fulfilment (Genesis 12:1–7; 15:1–6; 17:1–8). He was prepared to accept that God was working his purpose out, even when its first fragile fruit seemed to be under threat of destruction (Genesis 22:9–11). Abraham was already aware of the truth that with God, nothing is impossible, not even overcoming the finality of death (Hebrews 11:17–19). So, also, against all the odds Sarah believed in the promise of a faithful God (v11).

This kind of faith looks hopefully to the future and lives trustfully in the present. The ultimate goal is the full enjoyment of what God has prepared. Hebrews talks of this as a city and homeland to which believers truly belong (vv13–16). (He will say more of this later.) When they arrive there, God's people have come home. It is an experience to which the old covenant faithfuls could only look forward. For example Joseph (v22) anticipates in faith that God would return his people to the land of promise (Genesis 50:24–25). As Hebrews will soon make clear for new covenant believers, faith is more than anticipation. We do not have to live out the length of our earthly exile before we taste the joys of home. We belong in heaven – and Jesus has shown us the way to experience heaven on earth. Nonetheless, we have not yet taken up full residence. The need for faith is not yet redundant!

In the same way, neither is the need for faithful obedience. Here, too, we can learn much from the patriarchs. Obedience not only tests our faith, it also strengthens and builds it up. Even more important is the opportunity it presents to co-operate with God in the patient realization of his purposes.

The costly challenge of faith

Hebrews now stresses a dimension of faith that was of the utmost importance to a community in danger and under threat of persecution, a community strongly tempted to break faith in the interests of its own safety. Faith does not bow to oppressive earthly authorities, however powerful.

Faith, rather, trusts in the greater power of God. Such trust, vividly exemplified by Moses and his parents (11:23–29), can require a large measure of courage, for the behaviour it inspires may well lead to danger. Sometimes, indeed, it involves much human suffering. When believers have chosen to be on God's side and share God's life, they will not only know something of his joy but also something of the pain to which he is subjected by a rebellious and selfish world. Yet in the end, God will not be defeated. Neither, by the grace of God, will his faithful adherents.

Hebrews is in no doubt that the key to Moses' persevering faith was his perceptive relationship with God. He endured 'because he saw him who is invisible' (v27). Looking to the unseen God gave Moses the confidence and determination to carry on and to carry out the divine will. Not that he found it easy. Reading about his experiences in the Old Testament makes us aware of the personal inner struggles Moses had to go through in seeking to respond to (and avoid!) what God asked of him.

Coming to terms with what God wants to do in us and through us can be a decidedly uncomfortable experience. All too often God does not seem to see us and our situations in the same light that we see them. God's will can strike us, as it did Moses, as highly inappropriate. Yet, as we dare to look to God, we shall perceive a truth that makes all the difference: that all God's resources are at our disposal.

With the benefit of hindsight, Hebrews discerned that Moses suffered disgrace 'for the sake of Christ', thus reminding us that God's Son has always been with God (see chapter 1). Followers of Christ, however, have the advantage of clearer vision. When they look to the invisible God in their need, they see Jesus (2:9; 12:2). If only Hebrews' beleaguered congregation – and their successors – could realize that suffering disgrace for Jesus is, in reality, a high honour indeed.

Heroes and heroines of faith

The culmination of Hebrews' exposition on faith is nothing short of breathtaking. Fleshing out the Old Testament examples with references to other Jewish writings, he paints a verbal picture crowded with characters who radiated faith, often in the most adverse circumstances.

Some of these characters are perhaps surprising examples. Rahab, prostitute and outsider, is nonetheless commended for her courageous faith (11:31). Mention of her is a salutary reminder that God is no respecter of humanly-defined boundaries. He can work through the most unexpected and 'unorthodox' channels. We need the grace to recognize that when it happens.

Many of the people that Hebrews points to had to face appalling suffering (vv35–38). Some were rescued from it; others had to experience the full force of adversity. All of them held out for God's sake. Faith does not guarantee the absence of pain and hardship. Standing for God in a fallen world is well nigh certain to provoke hostility. But faith does open us to the strengthening and the understanding encouragement of God. Whatever our outward circumstances, God is with us, working all things together for good. That we can stake our life on.

The end of chapter 11 carries an amazing message. All these great figures of faith from the time of the old covenant, though commended by God and good examples to us did not receive the fulness of what God had to offer. This was graciously planned for us, the people of the new covenant.

If these former believers could exercise such faith without the tremendous benefits we enjoy, how does this challenge us? We should certainly thank God for these people and rejoice that, now, they too have been received into new covenant life (v40).

Indeed, 'the world was not worthy of them' (v38).

Two pictures

Hebrews vividly sketches two significant pictures designed to help Christians understand the true nature of their earthly pilgrimage (12:1–11). Both are drawn from experiences which would be very familiar to the original recipients (another sign of Hebrews' skill as a preacher!).

The first scene is that of a race, taking place in the midst of a crowded stadium. Serious runners need to be as unencumbered as possible (at the time, it was the practice for athletes to run naked). They must be disciplined people, single-mindedly determined to reach the finishing line. So with the Christian life. We must do all in our power to rid ourselves of anything that might hold us back in faithfully responding to God. We have our part to play. And our sights must be firmly set on Jesus, into whose arms we shall fall at the end of our 'race'. Jesus has run the race before us. He knows what it is like. He felt the pain of it in a way we shall never have to. And he will draw us towards him with his magnetic love. No distractions can compete with the prize he has to offer. Persevering discipline will be richly rewarded. We must remember, however, that in this race our aim is simply to make for Jesus, not to compete with one another. Jesus calls each and every one of us to go at our own pace. It is encouraging, too, to realize that we are being supported and urged on in our progress by a 'great cloud of witnesses': those countless faithful people of old whose 'racing days' are done!

The scene then changes to family life, discipline perhaps being the link in the preacher's mind. (Here he is very much indebted to the sentiments of *Proverbs*). Towards the beginning of his exhortation (in chapter 2) he has emphasized our privileged position as children of God. Now he underlines that part of this privilege is to be disciplined by God, prepared for mature Christian life, trained for heaven. At the time, this is often a far from pleasant experience. But discipline is not administered out of anger or malice. There is no abuse of power here. God's discipline is designed entirely for our good: to make us the people we have the potential to be, those who can share and live out God's holiness. Amongst other things, this calls for the development of perseverance – the determination to stay with God's cause even in the face of fierce hostility from his opponents. Standing firm against opposition (and feeling the pain of it) is something that God himself knows only too well. With his help, his children also can learn how to handle it.

Those who have had unhelpful and damaging earthly fathers (12:7–10) may need at first to approach this truth from a different angle. Put very simply: God loves us, and God will use every detail of our lives (painful or pleasant) to do the best for us and to bring out the best in us.

Living God's life

We cannot earn our salvation but we can co-operate with God in expressing the life of his kingdom. This requires a fair amount of hard effort. Hebrews now sets before his community a series of urgent and demanding imperatives.

They apply equally to any Christian community.

We are to guard against giving in to the kind of resigned spiritual weakness that leads to inactivity and despair (12:12–13). In God's strength we can get up and go, even if we feel none too steady on our spiritual feet! And we can make the going easier for ourselves and others if we work at smoothing the path ahead. Some of the things this might involve are clearly and dauntingly set out. We need to be peace-makers and peace-maintainers; we need to be holy (v14). Already we are faced with a recipe for effort, frustration and pain! Some of the most intractable and bitter conflicts take place within Christian communities, and are frequently all the worse for being covered with a veneer of charity. Such situations are poisonously destructive of the life and well-being of God's people.

Hebrews' warning about the capacity of bitterness – even in small quantities – to defile many, must be seriously heeded (v15). If bitterness is allowed to take root and grow, the effects on individuals and communities can be devastating. So too can the effects of sexual immorality – a particular temptation to a new covenant people called to deep mutual love (v16). In more general terms, Esau's fate demonstrates the grave consequences of putting the immediate satisfaction of desire before the long-term purposes of God.

Battling against temptation and the power of negativity, steadfastly walking in the way of God's commandments: such things are hard work. But in no sense do we have to tackle them alone. The key phrase in this section – 'the grace of God' – is something we can all too easily overlook, yet it makes all the difference to our situation. With grace, all things are possible.

Our true home

As Hebrews nears the end of his exhortation, he stresses yet again the privilege and responsibility of belonging to the new covenant people (12:18–24). Undoubtedly, this was a lesson his community needed to learn afresh – and take to heart. It is no less crucial for us.

First, we are reminded of the terrifying setting in which God inaugurated the Mosaic covenant on Mt Sinai. God's holiness blazed so strongly that the Israelites could not safely approach the mountain. By contrast, we who follow Jesus can freely approach the heavenly Mt Zion, the city God has prepared for us, our true home (*cf* 11:13–16; 13:14). We belong there, in that place of pure rejoicing, because we are sisters and brothers of Jesus, children of the living God, beneficiaries of the new covenant. It is a city, a kingdom, that cannot be destroyed, unlike anything else that exists. To quote Luther's hymn, when all else is shaken and tottering, 'the city of God remaineth'. That city is both our ultimate destination and somewhere we can (and must) visit, even now. How do we do that? By turning to God in thankful, awe-filled worship, joining in the praises of heaven and looking to Jesus with confident honesty and trust. This is something we need to do individually and together as Christian assemblies. It is our privilege and our responsibility. If we lose contact with our spiritual home, we shall not be able to enjoy and share its blessings. We shall be lonely indeed. If we are not able to meet together with other Christians, we can still enter frequently into the prayer and worship of the whole company of heaven. It is a privilege that God can use powerfully, not just for our good but for the good of the Church and the world.

Right at the outset, Hebrews proclaimed that God had spoken to us in his Son (1:1–3). He now warns us of the folly of closing our ears – and our lives – to God's word; a word costly both to God and to us (12:25–27). We recall that the word of God penetrates relentlessly into the very core of our being (4:12). Yet if we welcome God's voice as expressed in Jesus, we have nothing to fear. The fire of God's love (12:29) will warm our hearts and destroy only the dross in our lives.

Concluding advice

Hebrews' concluding advice (13:1–16) on Christian living repays careful pondering. He presents his community, and us, with a formidable challenge.

What is required of us includes: love towards sisters and brothers in Christ; generous hospitality to strangers; purity; strict faithfulness in relationships; a willingness to sit light to material goods and securities; wholehearted trust in God; and exclusive allegiance to Jesus, which includes our readiness to share in his rejection and disgrace. As if that were not enough, we are urged to a kind of prayer that is likely to cost us dearly. We are to 'remember' (pray for) prisoners and the ill-treated *as though we were sharing their experience* (v3).

Just as Jesus understood his saving work from an inside knowledge of the human condition, so we are called to 'incarnational praying': holding needy people before God, not with detached concern but with passionate involvement. Such is the Spirit's prayer – and only the Spirit can enable us to practise and to bear it. Such, too, is the way Jesus constantly intercedes for us in heaven (7:25).

And heaven is where we are bound. Again Hebrews

talks of it in terms of a city (13:14). Searching out this city means recognizing that any other dwelling-place is temporary. In our relationship with God we need to be prepared to move on, even from a place which has brought security and blessing, though what comes next may not, in human terms, be nearly so desirable. For the original recipients of *Hebrews* those truths were becoming all too apparent. In their time of crisis, they had to make a choice: break with the past for Jesus' sake, or retreat into a situation which could only, at best, bring short-term relief.

For them, the past was not a life of sin but a life of dedication to the requirements of God as set out in the Jewish law. This had a very holy attraction, a godly agenda, and was therefore all the harder to resist. It was (and still is) easier to take one's stand on religious tradition (of whatever description) than to go with the strange and challenging ways of the living and active God.

The imagery Hebrews uses in verses 10–13 would certainly bring his community up sharp! Its background is the prescribed ritual for the Day of Atonement, not this time in relation to the high priest's venture into the Most Holy Place, but to the disposal of animal sin-offerings (see Leviticus 16:27–28). These polluted carcases had to be taken outside the holy settlement of the people of God to a place of alienation and exclusion to be destroyed. They were unclean, unfit for any other use. The one who performed the task of dealing with them had to purify himself before he could re-enter the camp. Handling these corpses brought ritual contamination.

The fate of Jesus, says Hebrews, was like the fate of those animals (13:11–12). He was the sin-offering *par excellence*. He became a thing of disgrace, to be discarded outside the confines of the holy city. The body of Jesus was destroyed outside Jerusalem in a place of shame. The one who makes holy (2:11), the one who is 'holy, blameless, pure' (7:26), died an unholy death, condemned and rejected by the earthly representatives of holiness.

Where Jesus is, there his followers must be. The Hebrews community must take the enormous risk of identifying with Jesus in the disgrace he bore, as well as in the strange victory he won. This means facing serious consequences with effects that cannot be carefully calculated or controlled. It means leaving 'the camp' (13:13) and not going back. It means walking out from a community where they have felt at home, and being roundly condemned for doing so. It means being written off (and worse) as unholy, no longer fit for God or God's people. It means rejecting former understandings of holiness, which brought safety and protection – both physical and spiritual – for in the Roman Empire Judaism was a recognized and permitted religion. Following Christ carried no such advantage.

This is asking a very great deal. We can well imagine the questions and fears it must have aroused (yet again!) in the listeners as they struggled to come to terms with this sermon, and its message. 'Let us go out to Jesus,' urges the preacher, now reaching the final moments of his exhortation. 'Let us make that move, with all its difficult consequences. Only then shall we know the real joy of God.' Hebrews hopes that all he has already shared will have made his people ready and eager to respond with faith.

But he has not quite done. Building on the graphic imagery he has just employed, the preacher urges his congregation to a life of sacrifice. Breaking with the past is not enough! There has to be a continual surrender to the purposes of God. Though ritual sacrifices are definitely no longer necessary, there is still the need to make offerings to God, offerings that are more deeply meaningful. These sacrifices, though costly, are in no sense attempts to open up God's favour. That is there for the receiving. However, they can, as a willing response to God's grace, release much blessing.

What does this sort of sacrifice involve (in whatever situation we are placed)? It involves letting go of our self-centredness as we look to the welfare of others (v16). It also involves continually praising God (v15). That can indeed be sacrificial, for there are many times when we could not feel less like offering praise. When this happens, we can be helped by using tried and tested prayers and hymns of the Church as well as verses from scripture. We can also be carried by the corporate worship of the believing community. But perhaps the most honoured offering is that of persevering trust, honest prayer and determined confession of the name of Jesus when so much conspires to wrench us away.

Sooner or later we shall know in our hearts the truth of Hebrews' unqualified assertion: 'Jesus Christ is the same yesterday and today and for ever' (v8). And Jesus leads us on to joy and glory.

Grace be with you all

The final verses (13:17–25) contain some tantalizing and mysterious references to the author of *Hebrews* and his circumstances. Much scholarly detective work has probed into these 'clues'! What, for example, is the significance of the change from first person plural to first person singular between verses 18 and 19? Is the writer including others along with himself in verse 18? If so, who are they? Why does he feel the need to stress the conviction that 'we have a clear conscience'? And what does he mean by being 'restored' to his community? Is he in prison? Timothy seems to have been (v23). Could this add a particular poignancy to 13:3? How is Hebrews (and his community) linked with Timothy? And from where is he writing? When he says, 'Those from Italy send you greetings', does that mean that he is writing *from* Italy or *to* Italy (sending greetings from 'expatriates')?

None of these questions has anything like a clear answer. For those who want to explore them, the commentaries on *Hebrews* will supply many possible lines of enquiry. It is perhaps worth pondering that the preacher who has been urging his congregation to steadfastness in times of trouble may well himself have been in difficult circumstances. If so, his message would carry even more power. Like the God who speaks to us in Jesus, he would be speaking to his community with 'inside knowledge' of their problems. Rather than hectoring them from a safe and exalted place, he would be sitting where they sat. This would give added point to his consistent practice of using the first person plural form of address. He includes himself in his exhortation, not as a device but because he too is faced with crisis.

In the end, we do not need to know the writer's name or his background. What is crucial is to heed his message. It is as urgent now as it was at first. It faces us with the root issues and challenges of our Christian faith. And it assures us of the love, the power and the resourcing of the God who goes to extremes to claim us for his own. The intercessory benedictions of verses 20 and 21 are an excellent 'nutshell' summary of that truth. We could do little better than to make these verses a staple ingredient of our own prayers.

A note on leadership and the people of God

Three times in chapter 13, Hebrews refers to the community's leaders (vv7,17,24). Interestingly, these are the only times in the whole writing where leaders are specifically mentioned. It is well worth chasing this matter a little further, for it touches on issues which are still of considerable importance for Christian communities.

Even when, at the end of his sermon, Hebrews makes reference to leaders, he does not address them directly (*cf* 1 Timothy 6:11–21; 1 Peter 5:1–4). In fact, at verse 24, the people are exhorted to greet their leaders *on behalf of* the preacher. That raises the question as to whether their leaders are even present at their gathering. If not, why was this assembly taking place without them? Has there been some kind of breakdown in relationships? Or are the leaders, though contactable, prevented by their circumstance from being present? (Perhaps they are in detention because of hostile secular authorities.)

Certainly, it has to be noted that in the sermon as a whole the people of God are in much stronger focus than their leaders. And whatever the particularities of the context, such a focus is closely associated with the preacher's theological message.

It is the whole people of God, rather than simply their leaders, who are addressed directly by the preacher. He sees them as being in real continuity with the old covenant people of God. From God's people of old they can learn both what to avoid like the plague (disobedience and lack of endurance) and what to imitate with all their strength (perseverance and steadfast faith, even in situations of extreme testing; the willingness to move forward as pilgrims). And Hebrews is in no doubt that they bear the prime responsibility for their own pilgrimage. *They* are directly accountable to God. *They* must make their own decisions. *They* must take on the consequences of their faith (or lack of it). Whatever leaders are for, they are not there to lead people's lives for them.

This theme of the responsibility (and privilege) of the people of God permeates the whole of Hebrews' sermon. The people are beneficiaries of the new covenant. As such they are God's children: brothers and sisters of Jesus (2:10ff), members of God's household (3:5,6; 10:21). They are a worshipping community (12:22–24,28) looking to Jesus, the very self-expression of God (1:1–4; 12:2), who is both ahead of them (2:10) and right in the middle of them (2:12). Jesus joins in their worship and teaches them of God. Through Jesus, they all have direct and confident access to the presence of God. They need no intermediaries. They still have sacrifices to offer, but now they are sacrifices of praise and generosity (13:15–16), the surrender to God of a life of dedicated faithfulness (eg 10:19–39; 12:14–29).

They are to listen for God's voice in the present ('Today', 3:12 – 4:11), for they are living in the end-times, before his final coming (1:2; 9:28). This means paying close attention to Jesus, in whose life they are called to share (3:1,4). So they must be a pilgrim people, characterized by steadfast endurance and a willingness to leave the past behind. They are moving towards God's rest, their rich reward (10:35,36). Yet paradoxically, they can already experience this through prayer and worship (4:16; 10:19–22; 12:22–24).

The Hebrews community should be a growing and mat-

God of faith and commitment

uring people, developing the capacity to teach the things of God (5:11 – 6:2). They should hold together as God's family (10:25), encouraging and exhorting one another to love, good works and steadfast faith, taking responsibility for one another's spiritual welfare (12:15). Together they must be prepared for hard struggle, abuse and suffering, seeing this as part of their training to be like Jesus. Through their commitment, and the workings of God within them (13:20–21), they will discover eternal joy, they will come into their own, they will share the life and ministry of the God who created them for glory (2:5–10). They could not wish for a more fulfilling destiny. But they are free to throw it all away.

If the people of God have such a comprehensive vocation and responsibility, what place is left for leaders? From the references in chapter 13, it would seem that, for Hebrews, their task is committed oversight, setting an example and giving faithful and authoritative guidance. They are not endued with 'titles', like elder, bishop or deacon. The word used to refer to them is, quite simply, a description of function: it means 'those who lead'. There is no suggestion of hierarchy, of different 'orders' of leadership. And there is certainly no hint that these leaders are to be regarded as having special access to God. It is of no little significance that Hebrews does not describe 'those who lead' as priests. As he had made very clear in his sermon, this preacher sees the priesthood of Jesus as the priesthood to end all priesthoods. It is the expression of God's own priestliness. It can never be repeated nor imitated effectively. The only priest now needed to bring us to God is the one who lives for ever with God – Jesus. God's priestly life can be shared, certainly, but by everyone who looks to Jesus, not just by a separated few. (Hebrews does not speak of Christians as 'a royal priesthood', as does *1 Peter*. Perhaps he wants to avoid that term, feeling it might lead to misunderstanding. But he would agree that God's priesthood is shared by all believers.) Neither the old priesthood nor a *new* form of specialist priesthood is required. Both would be superfluous, not to say misleading.

So, according to Hebrews, what *is* the role of Church leaders? It is clear, first of all, that they are not to operate alone. In common with other New Testament writers, Hebrews speaks of a corporate leadership (all his references to leaders are plural). No individual has all the authority, nor all the responsibility. That is healthy. It guards against tyranny of various kinds, whether it be expressed in overwork, delusions of deity, abuse of power or the devaluing of others. The only person in whom leadership can be absolutely and safely vested is God, the one who leads to glory those who choose to follow. To God alone the people of God owe their allegiance. And so do the people's leaders.

Nonetheless, human leaders are not to be despised but honoured and heeded. At 13:7, Hebrews bids his community 'remember' their past leaders, those who spoke the word of God to them. They are to learn from these worthies and imitate them, for they were messengers of God in what they proclaimed and in the way that they lived. Their preaching was backed up by exemplary and faithful lives. The fruit of such lives must be examined over and over again (that is the force of the verb that the NIV translates 'consider'). Such examination should bring out a similar faithfulness in God's people.

Leaders, then, are those who communicate God's message in word and deeds, and in a way that brings out faith in others. They are to be good and encouraging examples. Verse 17 of chapter 13 gives us a further dimension. Leaders keep watch over those entrusted to them as people who will have to render account. The word used for keeping watch means, literally, going without sleep and staying alert (Mark 13:33; Luke 21:36; Ephesians 6:18). Those with oversight must be prepared to lose sleep over those for whom they are responsible! They also have to 'give an account' to God. They should be able to do this with joy rather than groaning (NIV 'burden'). 'Groaning' is a strong word and is used by Mark, for example, to describe the powerful spiritual and emotional activity going on within Jesus before he heals a deaf and dumb man ('he looked up to heaven and groaned', Mark 7:34). It is also used by Paul to describe creation groaning in travail (Romans 8:22) and the groaning of this earthly body as it longs for its heavenly destiny (2 Corinthians 5:2). For leaders to render account with groaning would involve suffering at a deep level before God.

But such a state of affairs would not let the community off the hook. Leaders might be accountable but they are not vicariously responsible. If an unhappy account were to be rendered, that would be of 'no advantage' to the people. They, too, would have to face the consequences. Hebrews' sermon will have left them in no doubt of that. They cannot shift the whole burden of responsibility onto their leaders. They must answer to God for themselves. They must also obey and submit to those who lead them. Though such 'authority figures' are most certainly not 'God', they have been given (by a means Hebrews does not specify) the task of overseeing and guiding God's people. They must be respected.

It may be that the Hebrews community had a particular

problem in this area. As we noted earlier, they seem to be meeting without their leaders. And they are in danger of drifting away from full-blooded faith. Perhaps in the light of their less-than-wholehearted spiritual condition, leaders were for them an irksome pressure to whom they were inclined to pay little heed. It is interesting to speculate how Hebrews himself may have fitted into the picture. He speaks with authority as one who expects to be heard. He is well-known to the community. He has a passionate concern for them. But he is clearly not one of their local leaders. Was he perhaps, like Paul, a travelling missionary who had a special connection with this group of Christians? Whatever the truth of the matter, Hebrews is concerned that the group's leaders should receive that obedience which can move the community forward together.

Those who lead have a crucial role in furthering the faithful pilgrimage of the people of God. They do so as fellow pilgrims.

7

OUR PRIESTLY GOD

Food for thought!

This sermon has undoubtedly been 'solid food' (5:12,14). By the end, those who first received it must have been struggling to come to terms with all its implications. Was there silence at this point? Did they continue with their meeting? Or did they begin to talk urgently with one another about the impact of what they had just heard? We can perhaps try to imagine their faces and their feelings. Profoundly disturbed, yet deeply encouraged? Experiencing the revival of hope, yet still fearing to rise to the challenge? This preacher has opened up so much. Some of the things he has said have hurt badly, but he has taken their situation seriously. He has met them where they are and given them a fresh vision of the living, saving God. He has strengthened them, put new heart into them – even though they are still reeling with the shock and wonder of it all. There are many things left to ponder on, to try to understand better. 'Infantile' he had called them. Perhaps he was right. His 'mature' teaching was certainly not easy to take in, but somehow he has convinced them that it is worth the effort. Severe and uncompromising he might have been, but his passionate care for them has hit home. How should they respond?

Such may well have been the effect of Hebrews' 'word of exhortation'. Of course, the opposite might have happened. The people may have reacted very negatively to a preacher who has exposed so much uncomfortable truth. It would be interesting to know the actual outcome but, whether positive or negative, the sermon is unlikely to have left its hearers unaffected.

What of us? Has the preacher encouraged us in our pilgrimage? Has he stirred up faith and made us eager to enter boldly into God's presence? Has he uncovered areas of believing and living that need closer attention? Or has he aroused a defensive resistance?

However we feel, he will certainly have provided us with food for thought. It is food worth digesting further. To change the metaphor, with hindsight and reflection we may be able to see the preacher's vision in sharper focus. It is fundamentally a vision of God. Hebrews discloses a picture which expands horizons and sees God from a different and daring perspective. This both challenges and heartens us. We may have to struggle with the detail of the picture but we shall be the richer for doing so.

At the heart of Hebrews' vision is the conviction that God has definitively expressed himself both creatively and redemptively in Jesus. We need to 'see Jesus' (2:9), fix our thoughts on him (3:1), 'fix our eyes' on him (12:2), if we are to deepen our understanding of and relationship with the living God. Hebrews has clearly done this himself. In the light of his contemplation (and his background) he has come to perceive Jesus as great high priest – a picture which makes sense of (and draws into itself) many varied aspects of his own Jewish Christian experience. It also opens his eyes wider to the essential glory of God. This was a vision he felt impelled to share, not least because he was convinced it was acutely relevant to the circumstances of his beloved community in crisis. We need to remember that context of urgency as we explore the vision for ourselves. Though it exercises our minds, it is no academic matter.

A vision of Jesus as our great high priest

With his insight into Jesus as high priest, Hebrews was breaking new ground. All the more important, then, to examine it closely.

The way to God
We need to recall, first, that the one whom Hebrews had come to know and worship as Jesus; the one who, as human being, suffered and died and was exalted to God's right hand; the one through whom he experienced forgiveness of sins; this one he had come to believe was none other than the eternal Son of God, the very radiance of God's being. In Jesus, God and humankind were brought together in a way that fulfilled the essential purpose and function of priesthood – a fruitful and eternal relationship between God and those made in God's image. To see Jesus as high priest thus brought into creative harmony the two main elements in our preacher's religious experience: its God-centredness and its focus on Jesus. Both elements are clearly reflected in his sermon. Both come together in the image of priesthood. In fulfilling his deepest purpose for humanity in Jesus, God has given flesh to the priesthood of his own being. We shall explore the implications of this a little later.

When we outline the basic ingredients of the priesthood of Jesus according to *Hebrews*, it becomes clear how many of them are carefully prepared for in the first two chapters of the Epistle. In summary, Jesus' priesthood has to do with mediating divine forgiveness, mercy and grace (4:14–16; 5:9; 10:12–18; *cf* 1:3; 2:3,4,9,17), with opening up complete freedom of access to God (4:14–16; 7:17–19,25; 10:19–22; *cf* 2:9,10), with enabling a 'heart-to-heart' new covenant relationship between God and humanity (7:22; 8:6; 9:15; 10:11–18; 12:24; *cf* 2:2–4, 10). It is characterized by self-sacrifice and suffering (5:8; 7:27; 9:14,26; 10:10; *cf* 2:9,10,14–15,18), by obedience, faithfulness and total commitment (3:1,2,6; 5:8; 10:5–14; *cf* 2:13,17), by a complete identification with the human condition which signals the will and capacity to help those in need (4:15; 5:7–9; 10:19–22; *cf* 2:11–18). Already, such features have burst the boundaries of the traditional Jewish priesthood. Not only have they 'perfected' the intention of that priesthood – to facilitate a safe human approach to God – they have also gone far beyond its cautious provisions. As a result of the exercise of Christ's priesthood, God can now be approached with *parrēsia* (boldness), as well as reverence and awe. And God can be approached by *all* who follow this priest. Jesus' priestly ministry is for all who will receive it. It is not restricted to members of a specially favoured people. The language and argument of Hebrews make that very clear. Jesus tasted death for everyone (2:9).

The terror of God's presence induced by human failure and sin no longer has any power for those who look to Jesus (12:18–24). Further, the perfection of priestly ministry turns out to have a deeply pastoral content, something not primarily associated in Judaism with the priestly task. It was the function of a Jewish priest to offer sacrifice (*cf* Leviticus 16:15ff; Ezekiel 45:18–20) and to give guidance and instruction in the Law (*cf* Jeremiah 18:18; Malachi 2:6–8). The care of 'shepherding' resided with the rulers rather than with the priests and was a responsibility delegated by God the supreme Shepherd (*cf* Ezekiel 34). It seems, though, that for our preacher, his experience of Jesus the priest-king, the 'great Shepherd of the sheep' (Hebrews 13:20), has caused him to look back at traditional priesthood in a pastoral light (see 5:2). Nonetheless, it remains true that the kind of 'sympathetic' ministry offered, according to our preacher, by Jesus would not have been available from priests of the old covenant. They were human, certainly, but it was not within their power to afford the sort of help offered by Jesus. He, knowing the full force of human weakness, expresses eternally and effectively that pastoral concern at the heart of God (*cf* Isaiah 49:14–16; 66:13; Ezekiel 34:11–16). Neither could they achieve *once for all* atonement and profound heart-cleansing. They sacrificed bulls and goats but not themselves. They were impotent to bring into being a new covenant.

The establishment of that covenant, as prophesied in Jeremiah 31:31ff (and quoted in Hebrews 8:8–12 and 10:16,17), was the direct responsibility of God, a fact reflected in the number of first person singulars to be found in the prophecy (nine in all). It is God who will make a new covenant. It is God who will put his laws into his people's minds and write them on their hearts. It is God who will be merciful toward their iniquities and remember their sins no more. How fitting, then, that the priestly mediator of this new covenant should be himself the direct expression of God in a way no other priest or high priest could ever be.

Neither could any other priest give the sort of guidance

and instruction associated with Jesus. For in mediating the new covenant, he is instrumental in writing God's laws in people's hearts (8:10) and bringing them to that intimate knowing of God (8:11), which is closely related to the profound purifying of conscience brought about by his blood (9:14,15). Deep inner cleansing prepares the way for a truer knowledge of God. That knowledge can only grow by looking to Jesus (*cf* 12:2), by being attentive to the high priest who can indeed reveal in his own person what God is like (1:1–3). Jesus does not simply give instruction in the Law; he discloses the God who is behind the Law.

The Law could make nothing perfect (7:19), neither could perfection be achieved through the Levitical priesthood (7:11), but Jesus the high priestly Son of God 'made perfect for ever those who are being made holy' (10:14). This last phrase is very important. It does not mean that Christians are all 'perfect' in the popular modern sense of the word. Hebrews is too much of a realist (and he knows himself and his community too well) to believe that! What the preacher is saying is that Jesus has made it possible for us to realize our divinely intended destiny of close personal relationship with God. That is our fulfilment, or perfection. As we take advantage of our access to God, God will keep working at 'sanctifying' us, making us holy (and that may well be painful! See 12:10). Jesus, then, brings into effect the new covenant of forgiveness and inside knowledge of God and his ways.

Interestingly, at 10:15 the prophecy of the new covenant is put into the mouth of the Holy Spirit. There is in our preacher's mind a close relationship between Jesus and the Holy Spirit. Each time the Spirit is mentioned, there is a significant connection with Jesus. At 2:4, the Holy Spirit's gifts bear witness to the truth of that great salvation, that new covenant 'spoken through the Lord'. At 3:7, the Holy Spirit, in prophetically proclaiming Psalm 95:7–11, urges God's household to be attentive faithfully to the faithful Son (*cf* 3:1–6). The reference at 6:4 is part of a severe warning that committing apostasy after having 'shared in the Holy Spirit' is tantamount to (re-)crucifying the Son of God. We are reminded in 3:14 that steadfast believers are described as those who 'have come to share in Christ' (the same word for 'share' as in 6:4). What believers share in is the divine life of redemptive creativity and rest in which Jesus and the Spirit are fully involved – the Spirit chiefly by witness and confirmation (2:4; 3:7; 9:8; 10:15), Jesus by giving it perfect human expression (1:2; 2:5–18; 10:5–14).

What is said about the Spirit at 9:14 and 10:29, however, points to a further dimension. The description of the Spirit as 'eternal' (9:14) suggests 'his' essentially divine character, whilst the phrase 'Spirit of grace' in 10:29, and in the context of the passage, suggests that the Spirit is integrally linked with God's gracious activity, in particular as demonstrated in Jesus. To insult this Spirit of grace by spurning the Son of God (the one who, by the *grace* of God, tasted death for everyone, 2:9) is to invite the judgement of the living God (10:29–31). These three (Son of God, Spirit of grace, living God) are to be thought of as being in very close conjunction. Indeed it is through God's Spirit that Jesus the high priest establishes the prophesied covenant and leads people into a heart-knowledge of God and his ways (9:14,15). There is no 'doctrine of the Trinity' expounded in *Hebrews*, but the preacher is undoubtedly moving towards the notion of threefold plurality in God, pushed perhaps by worship and experience rather than abstract doctrinal thought. Hebrews has certainly experienced in God a threefold reality – and this reality is focussed for him in Jesus. Jesus the great high priest, the mediator of the new covenant, is the radiance of God's glory and carries out his sacrificial ministry of grace through God's eternal Spirit. The 'problem' of trying to *explain* this theologically was left for others to tackle!

The same might be said of Romans 8, where Paul talks of both Jesus and the Spirit interceding for God's people (vv26,27,34). The preacher of *Hebrews* makes no mention of the Spirit's work of intercession but at 7:25 he does assert that Jesus the high priest 'is able to save completely those who come to God through him, because he always lives to intercede for them'. Here again, Hebrews is going beyond traditional Jewish notions of high priestly vocation. Many commentators explain his understanding in terms of advocacy (*cf* 1 John 2:1,2), with Jesus either pleading the cause of sinful humanity or articulating requests for help. The Levitical high priest was not particularly regarded as an intercessor in this 'verbal' sense. It is questionable, however, whether at this point the preacher is really thinking of intercession as pleading a case. The one seated at God's right hand had 'once for all' dealt with the sinfulness of the human condition. If God had ever needed any persuasion to forgive, he needed such persuasion no more. The whole point of the new covenant was the free offering of forgiveness and the enjoyment of free access to God (Hebrews 10:10–22). By his covenant sacrifice, Jesus 'has made perfect for ever those who are being made holy' (10:14). What need then for special pleading?

Further, the notion of pleading suggests a prior unwillingness on the part of God to release his forgiving grace.

Such a divine attitude, however, does not sit easily with the major thrust of Hebrews' theology. His opening sentence (1:1–4) sets the tone and points the way. It is *God* who has always taken the initiative in reaching out to his people; God who, in the one who is his Son, makes purification of sins. As we saw earlier, God does not need convincing that his people need his mercy. That mercy has always been operative and he exercises it to perfection in his Son. The relationship between God and his Son is one of utter unity: unity of person, will and authority (1:1–3; *cf* 10:7,9). The Son's prayer is thus God's own prayer.

We perhaps draw nearer to our author's understanding of intercession when we shift our focus to the giving of timely help (*cf* 4:16). The extending of such help is integral to the relationship of God with his people. The Jewish scriptures bear eloquent witness to that. The Son's human experience in testing and suffering, as it were, reinforces this divine ministry, for it makes possible a very direct identification with human need. The exalted Son brings into God's presence and God's experience the fulness of his human pilgrimage with all its consequences. The one who is the radiance of God's glory and through whom humanity was created now knows what it is like to live in a fallen world, and in heaven that knowledge is translated into his Father's awareness and active concern. Such is the weight of our great high priest's intercession.

No Levitical priest could match such prayer, though when the high priest, in the Most Holy Place, wore two stones engraved with the names of the tribes of Israel, he did point to its possibility (*cf* Exodus 28:9–12). Yet Jesus, the perfect high priest, opens the way for *all* to enter and enjoy the very presence of God. He is, therefore, not *just* a representative. He makes it possible for all who follow him to come into direct and intimate relationship with God, to share his experience. That, however, as Hebrews is at pains to point out, means coming to glory through suffering (*cf* 12:1–24).

A *focal understanding*

For Hebrews, seeing Jesus as great high priest took in various other ways of trying to express Christ's significance, and made deeper sense of them. It must have been an exciting moment when this understanding began to dawn – even more so, perhaps, when he realized what a difference it could make to a threatened and disillusioned community.

During the course of his sermon he seeks to demonstrate that his vision of the priestly Jesus is big enough to include and transform familiar ideas, big enough to draw existing perceptions together and express them afresh. By so doing, he hopes to bring his congregation to recognize how 'fitting' it is to understand Jesus as priest. Like the pastor and preacher that he is, Hebrews uses familiar ways of understanding Jesus, familiar expressions of worship and belief, to lead people into his new and broader view.

So in his presentation we, too, can discern a number of perceptions of Jesus that we come across elsewhere in the New Testament. But we find that these are consistently and suggestively blended together with the picture of Jesus as high priest. There is much material for meditation here, much to stimulate our thinking and praying.

One familiar and important understanding of Jesus taken up by Hebrews in this way is that of *mediator of the new covenant*. We find this idea also in passages such as Mark 14:24, 1 Corinthians 11:25 and 2 Corinthians 3:6. Nowhere else, however, is the Lord who brings the new covenant into being described as a priest. Only Hebrews makes that fascinating connection. He develops the theme of new covenant in some depth, especially in chapters 8 to 10. And he stresses how Jesus as its mediator is greater than those who mediated the former covenant (the angels and Moses). Crucial to the reliability of Jesus as 'the guarantee of a better covenant' is his status as divinely affirmed and eternal priest (7:21,22).

This is a most interesting contention, for not even a *high* priest was involved in the inauguration of the old covenant (*cf* Exodus 24:3–8). Yet it is clear from our author's exposition that bringing into being a new covenant was part of Jesus' *priestly* vocation. His high priesthood was not simply an additional feature. It was integral to his making possible a new covenant relationship with God (7:21,22; 8:1–6; 9:11–15).

That relationship involved deep forgiveness of sins and 'heart-knowledge' of God (8:8–12; 10:16,17, quoting Jeremiah 31:31ff). Such was the desire of God for his people. He had expressed this desire in the sacrificial system of the old covenant, most notably in relation to the Day of Atonement, making provision for the high priest to represent his people in seeking atonement for sin. Yet persistent human failure and weakness had rendered this provision imperfect and ineffective (10:1–4). It was this which no doubt encouraged our author to present Jesus the high priest as mediator of a new covenant. He saw this high priest as the full expression of God's desire for intimate communion with humanity (1:1–4), who in offering himself made both a covenant sacrifice and final atonement for sin (*cf* eg 7:15–28).

From his understanding of Jesus as 'priestly mediator' of the new covenant, Hebrews draws out the assurance of a new and close relationship with God based on full forgiveness of sins. From the notion of Jesus as the Servant (found at many points in the Old Testament), he highlights the significance of suffering, which is bound up with voluntary and redemptive self-offering, and leads on to exaltation (*cf* Isaiah 53). It would seem from Isaiah 42:6 and 49:6 that the servant figure is also in some way regarded as the mediator of a covenant of universal significance. So Jesus the high priest, infused with God's Spirit, offers himself (9:14), endures great suffering (2:10), bears the sins of many (9:28) thereby mediating a new covenant (9:15), and is vindicated and honoured by God (2:9). He perfectly fulfils the vocation of the servant.

He is also the new Adam. This is an understanding that can be found in a number of New Testament writings, not least in 1 Corinthians 15:21–28, where Paul uses Psalm 110 and Psalm 8 in a new Adam context. What is new in *Hebrews* is the association of this imagery (eg 2:5–18; 4:12–16) with the perception of Jesus as high priest. The human being who, in perfect obedience, resists sin and temptation can be our sympathetic and effective representative before God.

Of great importance for Hebrews (as for other New Testament writers) is the conviction that Jesus the Son of God is the King who sits at God's right hand in fulfilment of Psalm 110:1 (Hebrews 1:3,13) and whose throne is eternal (1:8). The characteristics of his kingship are righteousness and gladness (1:8,9) and the whole tenor of chapter 1 suggests that his sovereignty is universal, an impression reinforced by what is implied of Jesus at 2:8f. He is certainly a messianic king but this Messiah is also agent and ruler of creation (1:2,3; 2:8f), the radiance of God's glory. His divine, kingly glory, moreover, is not only expressed in heavenly exaltation. It is also to be powerfully discerned in the 'suffering of death' (2:9).

This paradox is, for our preacher, creatively associated with the high priesthood of Jesus the Son. For the writer of *Hebrews*, kingship and priesthood are vitally linked, for together they underline that inter-relationship between suffering and glory which he believed to be at the heart of the Christian message. Psalm 110 provided him with an effective vehicle for setting forward this combination of vocations. It was addressed to the Davidic king (and Jesus the 'Lord' was descended from Judah, Hebrews 7:14), yet verse 4 declared him also to be a priest for ever after the order of Melchizedek. No other New Testament writer makes this connection, but for Hebrews it expresses admirably his perception of the royal priesthood of Jesus.

The first direct quotation of Psalm 110:4 comes at Hebrews 5:6. After further preparatory references at 5:10 and 6:20, our author focuses attention on the figure of Melchizedek in chapter 7, drawing now on Genesis 14. His very name points to the significance of his kingship, for it indicates that he is 'king of righteousness'. Further, he is king of Salem and therefore, by translation, 'king of peace' (7:2). Melchizedek's kingship, then, has qualities characteristic of the messianic age – and his kingship is inextricably bound up with his priesthood. So, *par excellence*, with the Son of God to whom Melchizedek points (7:3). 'Our Lord', having arisen out of Judah (7:14), was indeed the hoped for Messiah King, bringing the blessings of righteousness and peace but, like the 'Lord' addressed in Psalm 110:1, he is also a Melchizedekian priest (7:15–28). And in respect of both he, as eternal Son of God, is true pattern and fulfilment, the perfect expression of the kingship and priesthood of God himself.

Psalm 110:1 is specifically linked with the high priesthood of the Son at Hebrews 8:1 and 10:12f. The latter occurs in the context of a passage which makes clear that Christ's kingly high priesthood was exercised in a most surprising way. The single offering, the 'one sacrifice' by which 'he has made perfect for ever those who are being made holy' (10:14) was none other than 'the sacrifice of the body of Jesus Christ' (10:10). Christ the royal high priest offered himself as a sacrifice, making possible full and final remission of sins and confident access to God. In this he was unique. No king had ever made such a sacrifice, not even the priest king Melchizedek, similar to the Son of God in so many other ways. Here is a bold new definition of the sovereignty of Jesus the Son. Bearing the very stamp of God's nature (1:1–3), he exercises his regal authority by an act of total self-giving which was both priestly and sacrificial in character (*cf* 10:5–22). That act was 'once for all' but his capacity to identify with and care for weak humanity is everlasting (*cf* 4:15; 7:25). Seated at God's right hand in kingly splendour is a high priest who longs that people should draw near to the throne of grace and who has gone to the most extreme lengths to make that possible. Moreover, this royal high priest perfectly reveals the attitude and activity of God.

Jesus as king was undoubtedly a familiar notion to our preacher. Jesus as high priest who offered himself was a new perception. Perhaps the representative character of both Jewish kingship and Jewish high priesthood helped him to make the connection between the two. In his understanding, Jesus was very much a representative figure, representing to perfection both his human brothers and sisters and his divine Father. In any event the connection made was a creative one. It is the kind of high priest Jesus is that provides the key to the nature of his kingship – a divine majesty infused with saving suffering. Such a faith-building paradox Hebrews urgently wished to get across to his community in their time of testing (*cf* 5:11ff).

Another way of seeing Jesus, which would have been familiar and is clearly of great significance for Hebrews, is as God's Son. For our preacher, at least, this is a relationship which stems from eternity, as well as being expressed in human history. It is proclaimed emphatically in the opening sentence of the sermon and is reinforced and further defined by the rest of chapter 1. Right from the outset of his writing, Hebrews is seeking to make a pregnant link between the Sonship and the priesthood of Jesus, a link which he hopes will develop and bear fruit as his 'word of exhortation' proceeds. So in his first sentence he refers to the one who is the Son having made purification for sins (1:3); and at 1:8–9 he uses, as spoken of the Son, a psalm quotation which anticipates the royal, righteous and eternal character of Christ's Melchizedekian priesthood.

All the eight references to Jesus the Son outside chapter 1 are closely associated with the nature of his priesthood. For Hebrews, then, the Sonship and high priesthood of Jesus are inextricably intertwined. Each sheds light on the character and significance of the other. Together they express something of great importance about the nature and activity of God himself. He who has spoken definitively in his Son has spoken in priestly fashion, giving flesh to his active desire to bring humanity into unhindered communion with himself.

Mediator of a new covenant, Servant, new Adam, King, Son: all these existing perspectives on Jesus are united by and in our preacher's vision of the high priesthood of

Jesus. But even taken together, they cannot contain it.

In the order of Melchizedek

By linking the priesthood of Jesus with familiar themes, Hebrews is seeking to prepare his community for a decidedly unfamiliar notion: that Jesus is not only high priest but royal high priest in the order of Melchizedek.

As we have seen in our journey through the text, the figure of Melchizedek contributes significantly to Hebrews' presentation of the priestly Jesus. It evokes mystery and occasions surprise. So does the priesthood of Jesus, which is not confined or defined by tradition (even tradition of God's own making) and breaks the boundaries of 'sacred' dynasty and race. Moreover, as prefigured by Melchizedek, it is eternal in character and efficacy, needing no dynastic succession. It is superior in status to the Levitical priesthood and involves the exercise of a kingship characterized by righteousness and peace. This indeed is a new way of looking at the office of a (high) priest.

In Jesus, claims our author, we have a high priest whose 'pedigree', though unorthodox, links him directly with God (*cf* 5:5–6) and whose sovereignty involves the ability to 'save completely [for all time] those who come to God through him' (7:25; 8:1–6). This high priest exercises his ministry 'in the sanctuary, the true tabernacle set up by the Lord, not by man' (8:2). His is not a limited and finite earthly priesthood (8:4–6), though it is infused with incarnate human experience (4:14–16). He 'always lives' (7:25) to bring about confident communion with God; and he can do this with complete effectiveness because he is faithful to who he is, the Son of God, 'without beginning of days or end of life' (7:3), who gives perfect and eternal expression to the nature and purpose of God himself (eg

1:1–3).

Though Melchizedek can point to this, he cannot himself fulfil it. Not even Melchizedek can take in our preacher's full vision of Jesus the great high priest.

It is who he is and what he has done that makes Jesus a high priest like no other. He bursts the boundaries of tradition and understanding. He can be seen in truest perspective when he is looked at in the light of God.

The priesthood of God

Hebrews' message about the priesthood of Christ is characteristically bold and radical. Christ did not inherit his priesthood as a son of Aaron, still less as a descendent of Melchizedek. He is a high priest because he is Son of God. His priestly character and qualifications derive directly from God himself (eg 5:5–6). His 'genealogy' is thus impeccable (*cf* chapter 1) and his priesthood the expression of God's own priestliness. It was as 'radiance of God's glory and the exact representation of his being' that God's Son 'provided purification for sins' (1:3). When we look at Jesus, we see what God is like. It is the nature and activity of *God*, as focussed in Jesus, to which Hebrews is drawing attention from beginning to end. It is God who has spoken definitively in one who is his Son. It is God whose voice we need to hear in Jesus.

What, then, does the preacher want us to learn about God and *divine* priesthood through its expression in Jesus? When we look at the various facets of Christ's priesthood as belonging to God, a striking picture emerges. This God, as ever, takes the initiative – and he does so in a way which both fulfils and surprises. In Jesus the high priest, he shows forth those qualities which have always characterized his relationship with his people: pastoral care and effective help, the mediation of forgiveness, mercy and grace, utter faithfulness and commitment, the exercise of kingly sovereignty in saving his people and the call for willing obedience from them. All these find their most complete expression through God's practice of his royal priestly ministry in Jesus. Yet there is much more to be said.

When God speaks as high priest in Jesus, he utters a word which, though familiar in many respects, is at the same time difficult and uncomfortable to hear, particularly for those from a Jewish background. It exceeds and explodes expectations of how he will act. Here is the God who reaches out to the whole of humanity, not just a chosen race, making possible for all people that intimacy of relationship with himself which had always been his intention and which was foreshadowed in the prophecy of the new covenant. God's desire to be 'fully inclusive' is heavily underlined in the sermon's overture (chapters 1 and 2), when the Greek word for 'everyone', 'all people', 'all things' is used fifteen times (1:2,3,4; 2:8 [three times], 9,10,11,17). It is particularly important in this respect to ponder carefully on 2:6–10. God has destined humankind for 'glory', that his human creation might share fully in his own life and sovereignty and know him 'from the inside' (*cf* chapters 8–10). To bring this about, he enters through Jesus into the human condition. He identifies with humanity in its fallenness, laying himself open to testing and suffering. He becomes 'victim' and is given over to death in order that his deepest purposes might be fulfilled and a new creation be brought into being through his travail (*cf* chapter 2). Such a divine high priestly ministry was unexpected not to say shocking. That God suffered in some way with his people was already a significant thread in Jewish understanding (eg Exodus 3:7–8; Judges 2:18; Psalm 34:18; Jeremiah 31:20). That he should make full and final atonement and inaugurate the new covenant by offering *himself* as sacrificial victim was not an action immediately thought of as appropriate to God. God's holiness and humankind's imperfection were incompatible, so much so that extreme caution was needed in any approach to the Deity. Yet the truth and importance of the incarnation – of God taking on flesh and blood – is something our preacher is passionately convinced of and which he seeks urgently to communicate.

God needs no intermediary to draw human beings freely and confidently into his presence. He does the job himself by incorporating humanity into his own being through and in the incarnation death and exaltation of his Son. For Hebrews, atonement cannot be understood, still less experienced, unless the union between God and Jesus is emphatically acknowledged. When God gives full expression to his priesthood, he does so in a way that perfectly brings together divinity and humanity, thus fulfilling the ideal of priesthood, breaking down all barriers and dealing for ever with the problem of sin. The at-onement of God and Jesus in the incarnation is the essential condition for the eternal effectiveness of Christ's atoning sacrifice.

It is God, then, who in Jesus the high priest makes atonement. There is no hint in *Hebrews* that this involved any conflict or 'transaction' within God himself. It is quite clear that the preacher felt there to be a complete unity of will and activity between Father and Son. The God who spoke with such redemptive creativity in his Son not only took the initiative, he remained fully involved throughout the enterprise of salvation. It is *God*, after all, who leads many children 'to glory' (2:10). His awesome holiness (also very real to Hebrews, *cf* 12:28,29) does not cause him to withdraw from sinners but rather impels him to take direct action, action that will make possible in humanity that holiness which enables men and woman to 'see the Lord' (*cf* 12:14). The holy God gets his hands dirty to make us clean.

The direct action he takes is to express his priestly care and activity in Jesus, and the way he does this points up his mystery and the 'unpredictable' character of his creativity. As we have seen, he breaks radically with the tradition he himself originated by not identifying himself with the Aaronic line of priesthood. His priesthood is prefigured by someone who is not even a Jew, let alone someone who has the right genealogical qualifications – someone who is on the edge of the Old Testament story. (We are reminded, perhaps, of God's consistent tendency in the Old Testament to make surprising choices.) This God cannot be confined or defined by tradition or expectation. He breaks down barriers and does new things. He calls people to leave the past behind. He acts in mysterious and shocking ways which can only be apprehended through paradox. The great and holy 'living God' (10:31), the 'consuming fire' (12:29), the one to whom vengeance (10:30) and judgement (12:23) belong, the one who demands absolute loyalty (12:25), makes himself totally vulnerable in his Son, makes himself 'victim' (9:11–14), identifies with weakness (2:17; 4:15), goes through death (2:14) and welcomes all into his presence with mercy, forgiveness and grace (2:10; 4:16; 10:17,18). All this because of the burning passion of his love. For Hebrews, this is the unified reality behind the paradox, and it can be experienced and entered into through worship, the authentic Christian worship which integrates reverence and awe (12:28) with complete boldness of access (4:16; 10:19–22) and finds its focus in Jesus (12:2). To know God in this context does not mean the end of searching questions. It does mean the deepening of a searching relationship in which tensions can be boldly explored and trustingly held together.

Such a perception of God blends well with Hebrews' characteristic approach of drawing diverse threads together to produce an inclusive and complex pattern full of suggestive variety. The high priesthood of Jesus he sees as the unifying 'theme' which for him incorporates the many-splendoured truth about God's self-expression in his Son. The major strands of his pattern he displays in his opening two chapters. As his exhortation proceeds, the pattern becomes increasingly involved and often surprising, requiring from his audience a fresh way of perceiving, a radical shift in understanding. What was familiar from both their Jewish and Christian backgrounds had to be looked at in a new light. Yet, at heart, the pattern radiates simplicity: God has revealed the truth about himself in Jesus his Son, and that life-changing truth can be expressed most comprehensively in terms of self-sacrificing.

This disturbing yet encouraging God will never fail us nor forsake us. On that we have his word.

SOME QUESTIONS TO PONDER AND DISCUSS

Hebrews puts his finger on many crucial issues with which his audience needed to engage. In various forms, those issues are still with us. The following suggestions for meditation and discussion may well open up further what God wants to say to you (and/or your community) within your own particular situation.

1 Hebrews highlights God's tendency to do new and surprising things, to challenge our deep-seated assumptions, to break with his own tradition, to take the past into the future in a way that both builds on and redefines it. Tradition is not God! We are graphically shown, therefore, the need for openness and attentiveness to this God: openness to change – radical, costly change – combined with a willingness to move on and see things in new perspectives.

How does this imperative challenge *us now*? What place does it leave for Christian tradition?

2 God has spoken to us fully and finally in one who is Son, in Jesus. All that Jesus is bears the very stamp of God's nature. As seen in Jesus, the priesthood of God is the heart of his life. It expresses God's costly and passionate commitment to reach out, to communicate, to challenge, to identify, to suffer, to liberate, to fulfil, to give his all

in merciful and profoundly cleansing forgiveness. God's commitment and faithfulness are total.

We can all draw near with confidence to this God, knowing that total honesty on both sides will be the making not the breaking of us. There is no further need of a specialist priesthood to bring us to this God.

How do we respond to the God of *Hebrews*?

What place is there for Christian ordained priesthood? If it has a place, how should it be understood in the light of the teaching of Hebrews?

3 For the preacher of *Hebrews*, worship and contemplation of a beloved (and alarming) God are primary. His theological reflection and urgent preaching stem powerfully from this source. He makes no apology for his assertion that committed openness to the God of Jesus Christ is the starting-point and end of his theological exploring. What, then, has his approach to say to us, in our debating and in the expression of our Christian worship, life and ministry?

In our prayers, thinking and discussion, we could benefit from taking to ourselves the prayer blessing of that anonymous and amazing preacher who has left us, by God's grace, the precious legacy of *Hebrews*:

> May the God of peace, who through the blood of the eternal covenant brought back from the dead our Lord Jesus, that great Shepherd of the sheep, equip you with everything good for doing his will, and may he work in us what is pleasing to him, through Jesus Christ, to whom be glory for ever and ever. Amen.

Another title from this series:

Encounter with God in Job
Dennis Lennon
Moving through the Book of Job, Dennis Lennon explores the powerful themes that arise from Job's predicament and invites us to use these as a basis for meditating on God's involvement in the painful moments of life. God does not abandon Job or condemn him for his doubts. Instead Job is given a deeper insight into God's love and provision for his world.

Both *Encounter with God in Hebrews* and *Encounter with God in Job* arise from series in the *Encounter with God* Bible reading notes. These series have been re-worked and expanded to book format but retain the distinctive *Encounter with God* approach to the Bible.